AROU
LAND'S END

First published 2004
by
LANDFALL PUBLICATIONS
Landfall, Penpol, Devoran, Truro, Cornwall TR3 6NR Tel. 01872-862581

Copyright © R.S.Acton 2004

A CIP catalogue record for this book is available from the British Library.

ISBN 1 873443 48 X

Every effort has been made to check that the information in this book is accurate, but the author cannot accept responsibility for any loss, disappointment, damage or injury caused by reliance on the directions or other details or statements herein.

Printed by the Troutbeck Press
and bound by R.Booth Ltd., Antron Hill, Mabe, Penryn, Cornwall

Typesetting, sketches, maps and recent photographs are by Bob Acton unless otherwise stated. The maps are based upon Ordnance Survey mapping on behalf of the Controller of Her Majesty's Stationery Office © Crown Copyright MC 100020399.

COVER PHOTOGRAPHS
Front: The coast near St Just, with the Crowns engine houses, Botallack Mine, in the distance (Walk 7)
Back, top: Porth Chapel beach, St Levan (Walk 3)
Back, bottom: Cape Cornwall from Kenidjack Castle (Walk 7)

TITLE PAGE
Granite formation near Land's End (Photograph by Stephanie Acton)

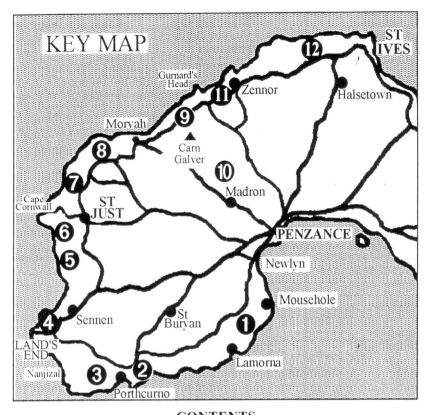

CONTENTS

USING THIS BOOK

I am always pleased to hear about people who buy or borrow my walks books just to read them and look at the pictures, but even more so when they tell me they've "done all the walks" - and survived!

The note at the start of each walk description is intended to be read before you set out: sometimes it would be useful to make preparations a day or two in advance in order to get the most out of a walk - for example, if you're including Levant in Walk 7 you might check first whether the preserved Cornish engine will be in steam that day; similarly, on Walk 8 you may want to visit Pendeen Lighthouse, and on Walk 2 the museum. The introductory notes also advise about parking, refreshments, toilets, the degree of difficulty of the walk, and so on. Bear in mind that my wife and I walked all these routes during winter, when mud was at its deepest.

The directions, which are picked out in **bold type** to distinguish them from the points-of-interest information, attempt to be very exact and explicit, but the maps are only fairly rough sketches, so I strongly recommend that you take with you the relevant OS map: most useful would be the "Explorer" Map No.102 (alias No.7), Land's End.

The technical terms concerned with mining are explained on pages 151-5. The lengthier notes about points of interest are printed in *italics*; if you are interested in such background information you might prefer to read them beforehand - or, as one of my regular readers tells me she does, save them till you take a hot bath afterwards!

I have done my best to ensure that all the recommended routes are on public rights of way, with a few unavoidable exceptions mentioned in the text, and that they are unobstructed. If you come across unexpected difficulties (new fences, changed field-boundaries, rotted footbridges...), please be patient, take the nearest practicable alternative way, and if possible let me know about the problem so that I can refer to it in any future edition of the book. Please help farmers and landowners by leaving all gates as you found them, and by keeping dogs on leads when there are livestock nearby.

ACKNOWLEDGEMENTS

The many publications old and new which have helped me in my researches are listed under Further Reading. Thanks are due to Justin Brooke, Kenneth Brown, Joff Bullen, Bill Newby and Graham Thorne, and especially to my wife, Stephanie, a native of Penwith, for sharing her knowledge, accompanying me on the walks and providing the picnics.

INTRODUCTION

Walking is good exercise (not for dogs only), and if you're lucky enough to live or take your holiday in Cornwall you have the added bonus of a beautiful landscape as backdrop. Like all the walks books I have published, however, this one is designed to appeal to those who want a lot more from the experience.

The points-of-interest information in this book is much more detailed than in any other "pocket-sized" walking guide to West Penwith currently available, but it would be impossible to do justice to every topic within this format. Natural history and geology are only lightly touched upon; the Further Reading section includes some recommended books about these. Again, because all but one of the walks are coastal, the important inland ancient sites such as Chun Castle, Lanyon Quoit, the Men-an-Tol and the Merry Maidens get no more than a passing mention. This is quite deliberate: I see no point in trying to compete with the work of Ian McNeil Cook, whose walking guides are the fruit of many years' devoted study of such features.

Those familiar with *A View from Carn Galver* will recognise that Walks 5-12 in this book are based on the routes described in that one, but all have been rewalked and revised as necessary - and I was surprised how much had changed since 1992. *Carn Galver* was subtitled *Mining Trails in the Far South West*; the fascinating and often dramatic story of mining in Penwith is a central concern in *Around Land's End*, too, but you will also find here the Iron Age cliff castles, the legends, the Celtic crosses, the holy wells, the churches, the watermills, the lighthouses, the shipwrecks, and much more.

I hope you will enjoy the walks, and find that the explanations enhance the pleasure.

Bob Acton

OTHER LANDFALL BOOKS ABOUT WEST PENWITH

A View from Trencrom covers most of the area between Penzance and St Ives and includes walks in St Ives itself and Hayle. Those interested in the history of Cornish mining will find the *Exploring Cornish Mines* series useful; and the history of St Ives, Carbis Bay and Lelant is told by local authors Lena and Donald Bray in *St Ives Heritage*. Further information about these and other Landfall books is on pages 159-60.

In memory of
Carolyn Trevorrow
who loved her walks in Cornwall

Land's End and the Longships
An engraving by R.T.Pentreath, 1830s

WALK 1
MOUSEHOLE & LAMORNA COVE

About five miles. If you base the walk on Lamorna and do not wish to include Mousehole, you could reduce the distance by nearly a mile and avoid one steep and lengthy climb.

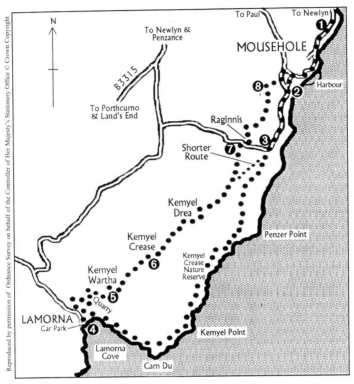

This is an attractive walk, and a fairly easy one, despite the fact that there are several steep climbs and descents, mainly on the coastal part. A little scrambling over or around rocks is involved, mainly at the Lamorna end. There is nothing to worry people nervous about heights, apart possibly from one short stretch on the descent to Lamorna Cove. At least in winter the path is likely to be very muddy in places, mainly on the return route through farm land and particularly farmyards. Susie Mitchell's *Recollections of Lamorna* tells of the postman's daily walk from Mousehole using the inland route here described: he crossed over fifteen "Cornish" stiles, she says - and they are all still there.

It would be worth taking binoculars, especially for the long view across Mount's Bay.

WALK 1

Mousehole and Lamorna both have public toilets which, as far as I know, are open all year. Refreshments are available all year in Mousehole, and there are a pub and a seasonal café at Lamorna.

Directions are given from the roadside parking area and pay-as-you-leave car park on the Newlyn side of Mousehole. Lamorna has a pay-and-display car park (free in winter); if you prefer to start the walk there, follow the directions from point 4.

MOUSEHOLE

The name, pronounced Mouzle, dates from at least the 13th century, and probably derives from a large sea cave south of the village: the OS "Pathfinder" map names it "The Mousehole". Several attempts have been made to suggest a Cornish derivation, such as "gull basin", Cornish "maew - holh", and even "Young Women's River", "mowes - hayle". Close by was another village named Porthenys, "island harbour", referring to St Clement's Isle, and by the late 17th century this name was sometimes applied to Mousehole itself.

The history of Mousehole goes back a long way, and to cover it adequately is beyond the scope of a book of walks: if you want more detail, try "Mousehole, A Brief History" by Margaret E. Perry, published by the author in 1998.

In 1292 Mousehole was important enough to be granted a charter entitling it to hold weekly markets, and there was certainly a quay protecting the harbour

by the 14th century. At that time, ports within the Duchy of Cornwall had to pay an annual levy based on the number of fishing boats: Newlyn was charged 10 shillings, Penzance 12, Mousehole 100; only St Ives paid more.

Fishing, the processing of fish - especially pilchards till recent times - and ancillary industries such as the making of nets and rope, have always been the mainstay of Mousehole's economy until their eclipse by tourism.

Ms Perry suggests that the 16th was "perhaps the greatest century for Mousehole", but it ended in a disaster from which the village (town?) never fully recovered. Seven years after the abortive attack on England by the Armada, four Spanish galleys anchored close to Mousehole (23rd July 1595). According to Richard Carew's account , published in 1603, some 200 armed men came ashore and proceeded to set on fire Paul church and the houses round about, including those of Mousehole, most of whose inhabitants had by that time fled. Within the next few hours the invaders had made similar attacks on Newlyn and Penzance. By the morning of July 25th, however, resistance on shore had increased and British naval vessels were approaching, so, as Carew puts it, "The wind no sooner came good, but away pack the galleys with all the haste they could." Neither Carew nor the commander of the four ships, in his account, gives a reason for these attacks: officially the expedition was merely for the gathering of information. If there was rape and pillage at Mousehole, it's surprising no-one says so.

With one exception, nothing approaching the drama of 1595 was to occur here during the next four centuries. Many changes took place, of course: for example, new quays, expanding and improving the harbour, were completed by 1870. The "one exception" was the tragic event of 19th December 1981, when the Penlee lifeboat, "Solomon Browne", with eight Mousehole men among the crew, went to the aid of a stricken vessel, the "Union Star", which was being driven by winds reaching 100 mph into shallow water just west of the Tater-du lighthouse. All those on board the lifeboat and the coaster were lost.

For many people now, the name Mousehole may conjure up first and foremost an image of its magnificent Christmas illuminations which attract thousands of sightseers every year; but the wounds left by those events over twenty years ago are far from healed, and the lights are dimmed in remembrance each 19th December.

1 Walk towards the village, passing the Old Coastguard Hotel. This road, The Parade, is itself part of the Coastal Footpath, and immediately past house No.12 it continues along the path on the left, which runs between houses and emerges at the small Harbour Car Park, where the public toilets are. The island just offshore is called St Clement's Isle, taking its name from a chapel which used to be there. The shelter the island provides helps to explain the early growth of Mousehole as a port. **Walk along beside the harbour, and in the narrow street beyond, where you pass the Ship Inn, a sign confirms that you are still on the coast path.** The Ship Inn is the focal point for the annual celebration of Tom Bawcock's Eve on 23rd December. He is said to have gone fishing in stormy December weather when no one else dared put out; he was given up for dead, but returned with seven different types of fish. They were baked into "starry-gazy pie", so named because the fish-heads stick up through the pastry, and such a pie is eaten at the Ship each anniversary. **Keep left at the junction. In a side road on the right soon after this is Mousehole's oldest and most picturesque building, still known as the Keigwin Arms although it is now a private home.** It is said to be the only building not burnt down by the Spaniards in 1595: its stone construction must have given it a much better chance of survival than the typical house of the time, with cob walls and thatched roof. Jenken Keigwin (pronounced Kegwin) moved here from Pendeen in the mid-16th century and grew wealthy in the pilchard trade. He is said to have been killed while defending his home from the Spaniards. His descendants, such as John Keigwin (1646-1716), a noted scholar who did much to preserve the Cornish language, continued to live in Mousehole, but apparently not in this house. In 1812 it was reportedly "in ruins", but by 1840 it was a pub, and it remained so till well into the 20th century. **Turn left again.** Notice the slate plaque on the wall to the left, commemorating Dolly Pentreath, a fishwife who died in 1777. She is often said to have been the last speaker of Cornish prior to the language's recent revival, but the plaque makes a slightly more cautious claim. Another Mousehole resident, William Bodener, is known also to have spoken and written in Cornish, and he outlived her by twelve years.

The route now returns you to the side of the harbour and then through another small car park (though this one is occupied by boats rather than cars, at least during the winter, and the toilets here were closed in November) **and past a row of cottages blessed with a wonderful view over Mount's Bay. Now turn right, steeply uphill, and from Merlin Place continue uphill, passing a coast-path acorn sign high up on a telegraph pole.**

2 At the T-junction, turn left and start the long climb up Raginnis Hill. If you find it a struggle, remember the nickname given to it by Dylan Thomas, who lived here for a while in 1937: "Raginnis-is-good-for-you Hill". (Douglas Williams included Dylan in a *West Briton* supplement entitled "Fifty Famous Cornish Folk" - but perhaps that's no more debatable than the Welsh poet's praise for Mousehole as "the prettiest village in *England*"! Mr Williams thinks *Under Milk Wood* may have been "inspired by Mousehole.")

Soon you pass, on your right, the Mousehole Wild Bird Hospital & Sanctuary, which became a household name at the time of the *Torrey Canyon* disaster in 1967. It was founded, in a very small way, in 1928 by Dorothy and Phyllis ("Pog") Yglesias, sisters who had moved from London three years earlier. (Their unusual surname is of Spanish origin, but there is no reason to think that any ancestor of theirs arrived in 1595!) The fascinating story of its growth over the years was told by Dorothy in *The Cry of a Bird* (1962, not long after the RSPCA took over) and *In Answer to the Cry* (1978, soon after the RSPCA decided to close the hospital down and the sisters came to its rescue). See also Alan Brunton's *Will I Fly Again?* (1993). The outside cages and gift shop can be visited daily (apart from a few occasions such as Christmas and New Year) between 10am and 4.30pm; admission is free.

3 After nearly half a mile (though it will seem more), where the 30mph speed limit ends and the road to Lamorna bends right, turn left through the grounds of Porth Enys House.

(The path on the right, signed Lamorna Inland Route, gives you an easier but much less attractive alternative. As my sketch-map shows, this is the path by which the shorter walk, starting at Lamorna, joins the coast path.)

The coast path for a while now is quite easy, level walking, and the scenery is mostly gentle. A ruined, overgrown building and several pairs of disused granite gateposts hint at the long-gone days when market gardening flourished hereabouts, producing mainly flowers and early potatoes. The cultivated plots were sheltered from the sea winds by tall hedges, some of which still survive.

Another reminder of past times is the forlorn little Penzer Point coastguard lookout building, its seaward windows now sealed up with concrete blocks. Despite much local opposition, most such visual watch stations were made redundant with the development of "high-tech" Coastguard Maritime Rescue Co-ordination Centres: Falmouth, one of six around Britain's coast, covers everything from Tintagel to the Dodman, plus 650,000 square miles of sea.

Just beyond Penzer Point the path descends very steeply. You need to watch your step carefully, but if you get the chance to look up you will see at least one substantial wall, evidence that the steep slope was once terraced by the market gardeners; such terraces were known as quillets. Judging by the fact that we found campion, violets and herb Robert in flower here near the end of November, this is an area plants enjoy, and a Clouded Yellow butterfly was busy among them.

The climb that follows is quite tough and involves some mild scrambling, especially where you cross a small stream and other boggy patches. At the top you come to the Kemyel Crease Nature Reserve, cared for by the Cornwall Wildlife Trust since 1974. A display board gives information about this "quite unique" site, a miniature forest consisting mostly of conifers, planted about a century ago to provide a windbreak for crops. Between August 2003 and April 2004 the Trust mounted here "an exhibition of natural sculptural environments", many of them witty representations of animals and birds, such as the one in the photograph; perhaps some of them will still be in place when you walk here.

Beyond the wood you get one of the best opportunities, in clear conditions, to study the panoramic view across Mount's Bay, which includes, from left to right, the Mount itself, Carn Brea topped by the de Dunstanville monument, Carnmenellis with its tall mast, Tregonning and Godolphin hills with the Great Work mine engine house on the ridge between them, Praa Sands, Porthleven, the Goonhilly Satellite Earth Station dishes and the wind turbines beside them, and finally the Lizard.

One final steep climb brings you to the view south-westwards from Carn Du ("black outcrop"), across Lamorna Cove to the modern (1965) Tater-du lighthouse and the Bucks, the dangerous rocks it warns ships of, with the Wolf Rock lighthouse tiny on the horizon. The descent to the beach at Lamorna is a long and rocky one, and in one or two places takes you uncomfortably close to the cliff edge, but it should cause no problems if you take it carefully.

LAMORNA

Lamorna is a beautiful name, and the place has often been praised for its "picture-postcard" qualities, but I have to agree with Des Hannigan that, at least as far as the cove is concerned, "its very popularity has diminished some of its charm." The garages, toilets, car park, café and row of rather sombre cottages dominate the beach, and the enormous waste tips of quarried granite which overshadow the scene are interesting rather than beautiful. The upper part of the beach is covered with sea-worn granite boulders (thrown up there, some say, by tidal waves caused by an earthquake in 1775), and in November these were half-submerged with soggy seaweed harbouring swarms of flies, so our plans to picnic there were foiled. Perhaps that explains why I am being a bit negative about such a famous place...

Its fame was created largely by a group of artists, one of whom, a man from Cheshire called Samuel John Birch who "discovered" Lamorna in about 1890

Lamorna Cove as seen from the coast path at Carn Du

and settled here, adopted Lamorna as part of his name. Keith Gardiner's list of "Lamorna Artists" (in Jim Hosking's book) includes 22 other names. One of them was Dame Laura Knight, whose account of her first visit here shows that it was the valley rather than the cove which cast the spell: "...we had suddenly entered Paradise: a densely wooded valley filled with lichen-covered trees of a greenish grey, whose branches threw a bluish tracery of shadow over the rich tufts of grass already speckled with the yellow of early primrose and white anemone." John Penwith wonders whether "Lamorna" might derive from the Cornish for "church by the sea", but there is no church, and modern scholars say the place takes its name from the valley: in the 14th century it was called Nansmorna, "nans" meaning valley and "Morna" possibly being the name of the stream, suggests Padel; Weatherhill's alternative explanation of the name is "blackberry valley". Another early name for the village, Nantewas, has been anglicised as "summer valley".

Farming, and especially the growing of potatoes, violets, anemones and daffodils for sale "up-country", was the staple industry here long before the dawn of mass tourism. Fishing never flourished as at Newlyn and Mousehole, which are far better sheltered from southerly gales. There is some evidence of tin streaming in the valley. The granite quarrying began quite early in the 19th century, when a certain Captain Owen opened a quarry on the western side of the cove; he built the quay there, plus cottages for the workforce and what is now the Lamorna Cove Hotel. (According to one account he built this as a house for himself; another version is "a hostel with its own little church for the quarry workers"; and a third is "the quarry manager's house with a

Carn Du in stormy weather: walkers beware! (Photo by Stephanie Acton)

chapel attached for the workers". Pity the poor writer of guide books trying to get at the truth!) Better quality granite was found on the opposite side of the cove, and in 1849 Freemans of Penryn began quarrying there. This granite contains many large felspar crystals, some of which take the form of a cross, and the workers used to sell small blocks featuring these as religious tokens. Among the places Lamorna supplied were the Victoria Embankment, the Houses of Parliament and numerous local sites such as the Wolf Rock lighthouse, and a 22-foot-long obelisk weighing 21 tons was sent to the Great Exhibition of 1851. The 6-metre-long block of dressed granite which forms the top step at St John's Hall in Penzance, which came from Lamorna, is said to be the longest unbroken granite block in any building in the world. Despite these achievements, the quarrying eventually became uneconomic; work ceased in about 1911.

Much of the seaward end of Captain Owen's quay had collapsed before that time, littering the beach with rock, and some old photos show an iron pier with cranes for shipping the granite. Susie Mitchell's little book tells how during the 1950s much of the cove and valley was bought by John Daniel, who had the quay repaired and removed most of the fallen rock.

Of course, there is much more to tell about Lamorna: the shipwrecks, the mermaid legend, the former watermill and waterfall in the valley, the Lamorna Inn (once a "kiddleywink" or ale house, and still known as The Wink), local writers such as Crosbie Garstin, Derek Tangye, John le Carré ... but I want this book to be portable!

4 **From the car park, return across the bridge, past the toilets and garages** (which stand where one of the quarry smithies used to be)**, and take the signed public footpath on the left, which climbs steadily up the eastern side of the valley.** This was used by the quarrymen and farm workers, and much of it is paved with granite. At the point where it turns right, it's worth

Lamorna in the 1920s. The cottage on the right was originally the quarry Count H(
(office). The large block of cut granite, bottom right, is still there. It had been desti
to go to the 1851 Great Exhibition, but proved too unwieldy to transport.

going out on the grassy platform on top of one of the quarry tips for the view of valley and cove. The most prominent building down there is the Lamorna Cove Hotel, which still has its small tower as a reminder of the chapel. **Not far past a ruined building on the right** (probably another former blacksmith's shop where the quarrymen's tools were sharpened)**, you come to the quarry itself (just one of three on this side of the cove).** The prepared stone was, says Susie Mitchell, "pulled and dragged with chains to the pier" down a short lane which has been totally "grown together" since about 1923; but in the last few years the granite was "taken by road through the Kemyell farm" (presumably Kemyel Wartha) via the dangerously steep hill down from Paul church to the stone-cutting yards at Wherrytown, Penzance, " on stone wagons drawn by horses." **From the quarry the path is signed to the left.** The abundance of stone slabs underfoot here perhaps confirms that this was the route to the farm for the granite, though the path is surprisingly narrow if so. **5 On reaching Kemyel Wartha farm** ("Kemyel" has been explained as "Michael's hedge"; "Wartha" means "higher") **turn right, and continue among several buildings - some dilapidated, others restored and/or**

The quarry on the walk route as you leave Lamorna

converted - till you reach a stone stile accompanied by a public footpath sign. Cross, then keep to the left side of the field. The path from here is fairly straight, its route marked by a succession of stone stiles; just before reaching Kemyel Crease (Middle Kemyel) farm you cross a fairly large field. One last stile brings you to a metalled lane.

6 Turn left on that, and shortly before reaching the last house cross a small stone stile beside a farm gate on the right, where there is a footpath sign. Now keep beside the hedge on the left and cross another small stone stile. The path now takes you through a boggy area, and after another stile there is a granite footbridge. As you approach Kemyel Drea (Kemyel home farm: "drea" is apparently a form of "tre"), a yellow arrow directs you half-left, where the path wanders rather vaguely through another somewhat marshy area.

Cross the farm lane to the point, more-or-less opposite, where you are directed to pass along a narrow passage between farm buildings, via several stiles and gates, the last of which looked like an old wooden pallet. Beyond that, the path theoretically continues straight ahead, but in November the deep mud, churned up to liquid sludge by cattle, compelled anyone not wearing wellies to make a detour to the left. Rejoin the path where there is another stone stile - easy to find because an old stone cross of the "latin" type stands beside it. This cross appears to have been moved quite recently from the position shown on the OS "Pathfinder" map, north of this place, where it still was when Andrew Langdon wrote *Stone Crosses in West Penwith* (1997). Now again the path is clear: fairly straight and marked by a series of stone stiles. The second stile (not counting the one beside the cross) comes at the end of a long field, then it is only about 50 yards to the third one.

If you started this walk at Lamorna and don't want to go down into Mousehole, turn right after crossing this third stile. Now you go diagonally across this small field, and after crossing three more stone stiles you will reach the coast path just west of point 3 on the map. Turn right to return to Lamorna.

To complete the walk which started at Mousehole, go on ahead. After two more stiles, the path goes across the centre of a fairly large field - not to the far corner, but to another stile at the end of a new-looking stone wall a little further left. Steps down from this bring you to a road.

7 Turn right on the road, then almost immediately left to pass among the various buildings at and around Raginnis Farm (*rag enys* in Cornish, "opposite the island", referring presumably to St Clement's Isle). The history of Raginnis is explored by Gillian G.Green in *Three Hundred Years on Penwith Farms*, published by the Penwith Local History Group in 1994. **Continue to the end of the lane, cross the stone stile there, and cut across the left-hand corner of the field to another stile, beyond which the path is clear, leading to yet another.** After crossing that you are in one of the fields where some of the famous Mousehole Christmas lights are set up: in November 2003 a big construction was already in place with Xmas and New Year greetings, and another depicting Christmas pud. At any time of year you can see Paul church from here, up to the left as you descend towards the houses of Mousehole. **A little wooden gate at the bottom of the field is followed by steps down to a lane.**

8 Turn left on that, and after about 20 yards take the narrow path down on the right, with a small stream on the left which is eventually culverted under the streets and houses.

It's difficult to give directions through the many little streets, and in any case it's hardly necessary to do so. Continuing more-or-less straight ahead is likely eventually to bring you to Fore Street, where a right turn leads to the harbour, from which retrace your earlier steps to The Parade and your car.

WALK 2
PORTHCURNO, PENBERTH AND TREEN
About three and a half miles

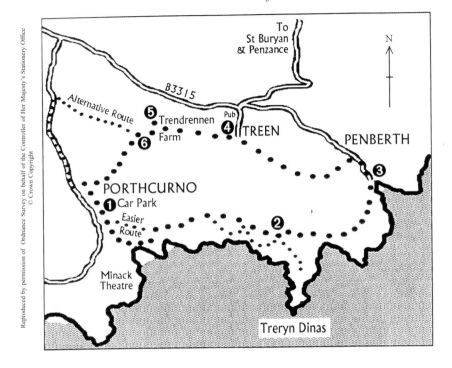

This delightful short walk includes spectacular cliff scenery - notably one of Cornwall's most awe-inspiring headlands - and a fishing village which, having been owned by the National Trust for many years, retains much of its original character. Porthcurno itself, with its fine white beach consisting largely of seashell fragments, the Museum of Submarine Telegraphy and the Minack Theatre, has more than enough on offer to occupy you all day, but I hope you'll manage to fit this walk in. Most of this section of the coast path is rough underfoot, and the inland part of the route is likely to be muddy in places. You would be well advised to wear good walking boots, especially if you want to explore the seaward part of the headland.

Porthcurno has a shop and pub (the Cable Station Inn); most if not all of the other "facilities" there, including the toilets at the big main car park, are available only during the season. Treen has a small shop and a pub (the Logan Rock), plus toilets which appear to be open all year.

The walk starts and ends at the Porthcurno pay-and-display car park.

WALK 2

PORTHCURNO

Modern students of Cornish place-names have concluded that this one derives from "porth cornu", "cove of horns or corners". Craig Weatherhill suggests that the "horns" are "the peculiar cliff formations there".

The alternative explanation, "Porth Kernow", port or harbour of Cornwall, is misleading, because the cove has never been used as a landing place by large ships. Strange as it may seem, this very fact helps to explain why Porthcurno became "the home of cable telegraphy" and thus a vital centre of international communications. The first company to bring ashore a submarine telegraph cable at Porthcurno, in 1870, was misnamed the Falmouth, Gibraltar and Malta Cable Company: they decided against Falmouth because of the risk that large vessels in a busy port might damage the cable.

That first cable linked Porthcurno not just with Malta but as far afield as Bombay and eventually Australia. In 1872 the four small concerns sharing responsibility for that line amalgamated to form the Eastern Telegraph Company. The story of the proliferation of cables at Porthcurno; of the growth of the college set up in 1870 to train operators; and of the fierce rivalry between the cable and radio companies early last century, which was resolved in 1928 by the creation of the body that came to be named Cable & Wireless Ltd: all this and more is well told in various publications, such as John Packer's "The Porthcurno Handbook" and "The Porthcurno Story", a colourful booklet published by the Museum of Submarine Telegraphy.

Perhaps most interesting of all is what happened here early in World War 2. Following the fall of France in June 1940, the need to protect Porthcurno from attack became urgent. 200 Cornish tin miners supervised by experts from further afield were set to work to create two linked tunnels under the hill just inland from the beach, with blast-proof steel doors at each entrance and a steep escape route consisting of 119 steps. The massive job was completed in ten months, and finally all the necessary wiring and equipment for the new underground communication centre were installed. For a vivid account of this operation, see "Cornish War and Peace" by Viv Acton and Derek Carter.

During the 1950s technological advances led to the gradual decline of cable telegraphy. To quote Mr Packer, in 1970 "the last telegraph circuit closed and Porthcurno ended, at least temporarily, its life as a link in world communications." 25 years later, however, Acton and Carter wrote, "It is still the landfall for international cables and in late 1996 the longest-ever marine cable, linking Porthcurno with Japan, will become operative." That quarter-century also saw the continued expansion of the college, and the conversion by a team of enthusiasts of the disused tunnels into a museum of submarine telegraphy, featuring early equipment collected from far and wide.

By the mid-1990s, Cable & Wireless had withdrawn from Porthcurno, handing over much of its property there to the National Trust and relocating the college to Coventry. Thanks largely to the efforts of the Trevithick Trust, the historical collection remains in the tunnels and has been further enhanced. The former college building - which for a time after the departure of Cable & Wireless was used as a training centre for the oil, gas and petro-chemical industries - has now become part of the museum. Late in 1999 the museum won the National Heritage/NPI Award for the Best Museum of Industrial History. Its opening times are from 10am to 5pm: every day in July and August; every day except Saturday, apart from bank holiday Saturdays, for the rest of the period from April to the end of October. From November to the end of March it opens only on Sunday and Monday. (These are 2003 details; for an update, ring 01736 - 810966 or 810478.)

The other big attraction at Porthcurno is, of course, the Minack Theatre. For information about that, see Walk No.3.

Porthcurno's main contribution to Cornish myth and legend lies in the tale of the ghost ship, a four-masted vessel which on misty evenings would sail inland as far as St Levan, says Judith Cook - much further, to Chegwidden, says Craig Weatherhill. Seek out their books if you want the story in full.

1 **From the seaward end of the car park, take the path signed Porthcurno Beach and Coast Path. After about a hundred yards you will see two paths on your left; the first runs back to the Museum, and the second goes uphill, eventually reaching the clifftop. Although quite steep, it makes an easier start to the walk than the official Coast Path; the latter is a bit of a scramble in places, and may be unnerving for those afraid of heights, but of course gives splendid views over the beach and along the coast westwards. The choice is yours! If you decide on the Coast Path, go on down towards the beach till you come to the National Trust Porthcurno sign; beside it is an inscribed granite block, on which you may be able to decipher the direction left to Penberth.**

The path is wide at first, but soon narrows and climbs steeply among granite boulders and outcrops; the little concrete seat about half-way up will probably offer a welcome rest and a chance to enjoy the scenery in comfort. Near the top is one of several "pillboxes" at Porthcurno (another can be seen on the far side of the cove), reminders of the importance of any potential landing-places along this coastline during World War 2. At the top, the view ahead is of the impressive Treryn Dinas headland. Now the path wends its way further inland, and **just past the National Trust Porthcurno sign is a low stile, at the point where the easier path mentioned above comes in from the left. Cross the stile and turn right.**

Soon you pass between two more "pillboxes". The side path on the right not far beyond them gives much better views than the main one, which stays quite well inland for a while. The side path runs close to a white pyramid, placed here by the National Trust as a navigation aid during the 1950s. The story behind it is told by J.E.Packer in his *Porthcurno Handbook*. In 1880 a French telegraph company brought ashore here its cable linking Britain, France and Nova Scotia. In the sheer cliff-face below are two masonry-lined channels, so apparently there were two cables. These were taken to a small wooden hut, from which a landline connected them to a telegraph office in Penzance. By 1930 the Eastern Telegraph Company had taken over this link and diverted the cables to Porthcurno beach, so the hut became dilapidated, but remained a useful navigation aid until the NT removed it, later substituting the white pyramid.

At the junction where this path eventually rejoins the official one (and where a wider track heads left for Treen village), another such side path is again well worth taking, especially for the breathtaking view near the start. Back on the main path once more, you soon reach **a second junction (point 2 on the sketch map); here the path going fairly sharply left is another link to Treen; the widest one, heading slightly to the right, leads out to Treryn Dinas; and the coast path to Penberth is the one in the middle.**

Even if you don't want to go right out on to the headland, the path towards it is a must for the splendid views, extending on the right side as far as the Bishop's Rock lighthouse, and on the left all the way across Mount's Bay to Lizard Point. You may be able to see the intermittent flashes from the Lizard lighthouse. Much closer is the small lighthouse at Tater-du, just this side of Lamorna. From the flat top of the inland part of the headland you can look down the steep, rocky slope to the narrow neck, beyond which are the great granite crags, aptly described by Craig Weatherhill as "resembling ruined turrets and battlements". Among them, on the west (right) side, is the famous Logan Rock. I leave it to you to decide whether to venture along the steep and narrow paths leading out there; it's certainly not advisable unless you are agile and equipped with the right kind of footwear.

WALK 2
TRERYN DINAS & THE LOGAN ROCK

"Treryn" is simply a version of the name of the nearby village, Treen, which means "farm by a fort"; "Dinas", a fairly recent addition, merely repeats "fort". The Iron Age cliff castle here is one of the most impressive in Cornwall. Four man-made barriers defended it, the longest and tallest of which is the embankment, about 300 yards long, through which the path passes immediately beyond the junction described a few lines back. A ditch ran along the north side of it. Two more ramparts with ditches defended the flat area. I guess this was the main part of the settlement itself, although the remains of two hut circles have

This illustration of part of the
cliff castle was made by
J.T.Blight in about 1870.

been found beyond the final line of defence, the ditch and stone wall which cross the narrow neck. For more detail, including a clear map of the site, see Craig Weatherhill's "Belerion".

The old name of the Logan Rock was "Men Amber", balance stone; "Logan" comes from a dialect word, "logging", meaning "rocking", so strictly it should be pronounced as "logg'n" rather than "low-gun". Cornwall has several such stones, created by erosion over many millennia. This one, said to weigh 70 tons, is the best-known, largely because of a famous incident in 1824. Responding to a claim by the 18th-century antiquary William Borlase ("It is morally impossible that any lever, or indeed force however applied in a mechanical way, can remove it from its present situation."), a Royal Naval Lieutenant called Hugh Colvill Goldsmith and some of the crew of his ship managed rock it sufficiently for it to slip about three feet and lodge in a crevice. (Certainly not "on to the beach below", as Judith Cook relates.) The action caused such outrage among local residents - especially the guides whose income was now threatened - that the culprit decided to replace the stone. (Some accounts say that the Admiralty ordered him to do so.) Luckily, he and/or his friends had the expertise to achieve this, with the aid of an impressive array of shear-legs, capstans, pulleys, blocks and chains. Young Goldsmith's bill came to £130.8s.6d, which included 13/6 (67½p) on account of "60 men *of St Just who did nothing but drink beer."* He was assisted by grants from the London Geological Society and the Cornish historian Davies Gilbert. When Cyrus Redding saw the stone in about 1840, it was, he says, "regularly chained and padlocked up, when the keeper is not near." It is often said that despite all the Lieutenant's efforts the stone never rocked again, but Mr Weatherhill explains how it can be set in motion, should you wish to try.*

It's no surprise that Treryn Dinas should be the object of numerous myths and legends. A giant created the cliff castle, another (the deaf-and-dumb Den an Dynas) defended it, and the Small People still tend their gardens among the rocks, playing wonderful music. King Arthur is said to have owned the headland, and witches used to perch on Castle Peak to conjure storms and other disasters.

2 The coast path from here is quite narrow and rough. It soon drops to a wooden footbridge over a stream above a small cove (Haldinas, "marsh by the fort"). After passing above a deep chasm, the rocky path climbs to the top

Typical scenery around the cliff castle

of Treen Cliff, from which the view seaward again extends to the Lizard, and inland to St Buryan church. Next comes one last steep descent, giving a good bird's-eye view of Penberth.

PENBERTH

The village's name derives from the Cornish for "end of the thicket or brake", referring to the well-wooded valley leading down to the cove.

Penberth is probably the nearest thing in Cornwall to an authentic, unspoilt fishing village; Porthgwarra and Cadgwith come close, of course, and so does Port Isaac, though the last is hardly a village. The fact that Penberth has been owned by the National Trust for almost half a century might lead to the conclusion that it has been preserved in aspic as a quaint museum piece, but in the Trust's "Coast of Cornwall" leaflet Des Hannigan puts great stress on the fact that "the cove still supports an active fleet of at least a dozen small boats, well equipped with modern electronics and manned by fishermen renowned for their traditional skills and seamanship." Admittedly, the impressive wooden capstan, renovated in 1997, is now for display only, and a modern winch does the actual hauling work. The pilchard cellars, well seen from the cliff path as you descended, have also been renovated, but still serve various practical purposes for the fishermen. My own mental picture of

The restored capstan at Penberth

Penberth is dominated by bold and enterprising cats, well-versed in the art of securing titbits from walkers' picnics - much like cats in fishing communities everywhere.

Author and cats

3 Leave Penberth by the road, passing a pretty stone footbridge over the stream. Where the road divides, keep to the lower alternative, on the left. Beyond the large thatched house, the road crosses the stream and widens sufficiently to allow car parking. Take the signed path on the left here. At first it doubles as the drive to the house ahead, but after the left turn it is narrower as it passes through a marshy area where massive growths of gunnera thrive. As with many such Cornish coastal valleys, the microclimate here is in great contrast with the surrounding landscape. **At the division of ways turn right, uphill, and then again right at the next junction.** The path was deep in fallen leaves in November, and here and there we had to step around bits of fallen timber. **At the top of the slope is a wooden stile, and the path ahead is clear.** Among the trees over to the right are a few television aerials, presumably serving the houses down in the valley. **After a stone stile, the path keeps to the top (left) edge of a field at first, then continues in the same line.** The impressive single-storey house below, with its own tennis court, is Penberth House or Foxstones, noted for its unusual 5-acre garden, which spreads up the hillside behind. (What is known as the Penberth Cross was discovered near the stream in 1920 and set up beside the drive in the garden. It has the usual wheel-head shape but appears to be unfinished, because no cross is carved on it. Andrew Langdon states that "there is sometimes access to the public when the gardens are open.") **The path passes through an open gateway, then comes a stone stile. As indicated by the**

yellow waymark arrow, you now turn right, then left, around the edge of a field. After a short stretch between wire fences, cross a wooden stile and turn right, into Treen village. Continue along the road, past the toilets and shop. The villagers here were, it's said, once so dependent on income from tourists wanting to visit the rocking stone at Treryn Dinas that when Lieutenant Goldsmith dislodged it, Treen was nicknamed "The Deserted Village", alluding to the poem by Oliver Goldsmith, the vandal's uncle.

4 To continue the walk, take the signed path on the left (but if you want to call at the Logan Rock Inn, go on past Treen Farm first). The path is clearly signed at first: it turns right immediately beyond the house, continues along a farm track, and then keeps to a fairly straight line via several stone or wooden stiles. As you approach farm buildings (Trendrennen) you can cut across the last field to the stone stile on the right of a farm gate, rather than walking around the field edge.

5 Having crossed the stile, turn left along the farm track, cross the stile on the left of the next farm gate and turn right. Keep to the right-hand edge of the field at first.

6 Where the field boundary diverges to the right, take a 90-degree left turn*(see note below), heading across the centre of this quite large field, towards an open gateway. Beyond that, the path continues ahead along what looks like an old tractor track. A dilapidated stone stile at the next field boundary has a waymark yellow arrow directing you to go on in the same line, across what in November 2003 was a ploughed field, and through an open gateway with a very overgrown stile on the right. The path beyond that is clear; it meanders a little, passing close to a wireless mast, and brings you to a farm gate with a gap on the right for the slim to squeeze through, and then you descend to the houses of Porthcurno. You could go on down to the road and turn left, but if the gate to the Museum, on your left, is open, that's a better way, even if you don't intend to visit the Museum. Take the steps down on the right and follow the path running beside the Museum's car park to return to your car.

*Please note that there is (or was, in November 2003) no sign to indicate where this path begins. If you miss it - as we did first time - you could continue ahead, following the yellow arrows. This will eventually bring you down to the road a little way north of Porthcurno's village shop. Turn left for the car park.

WALK 3
PORTHCURNO, PORTHGWARRA, NANJIZAL & ST LEVAN
About six and a half miles.
Two shorter walks based on Porthgwarra are also suggested.

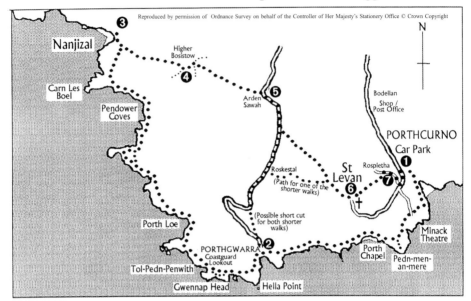

This is a magnificent walk, offering superb coastal scenery and plenty of historical interest. The coastal stretch is tough in places, with several steep climbs and descents; a good few paths and minor roads lead inland along the way, so with the aid of the relevant 2½-inch map you should not have too much difficulty finding a shorter route back to Porthcurno. (The two walks based on Porthgwarra are described at the end of this introduction.) Those walkers who do make it from Porthcurno to Nanjizal can take comfort from the fact that the inland return section is a good deal shorter and much less strenuous. The cliff-edge paths could be a problem for those with little head for heights, but the official coastal footpath mostly stays quite well inland of them. Paths and stiles are generally well maintained.

There is a shop at Porthcurno, though not on the walk route; refreshments are available nearer the beach during the season. The Cable Station Inn is close to the car park. At Porthgwarra there is a small shop / tea-room selling pasties, sweet pastries, drinks, etc; it is open daily from the start of April till the end of October, except when the weather is particularly bad. Porthcurno and Porthgwarra have public toilets (seasonal) and phone boxes.

Directions are given from the large car park at Porthcurno.

There is also a pay-and-display car park at Porthgwarra, so one easy way to shorten the walk would be to start there (point 2 in the directions). You could then walk to Nanjizal, following the directions as far as point 4, line 3, finally returning along the road; at the sharp right turn you could reduce the distance by taking the lane straight ahead, where there is a warning to motorists that this is not a through road. It eventually becomes a footpath which leads down to the cove. Alternatively you could make for Porthcurno by taking that inland path, which is clearly signed where it leaves the coast path, on the east side of the cove: turn left immediately beyond the cottage. On joining the road, continue ahead for about a quarter of a mile, then take the signed path on the right at Lower Roskestal farm. This is a tractor track at first, but later narrows to a footpath. Eventually, where you come to a stone stile on the left with an old Cornish cross among the stones on the left side, it joins the route of the full walk near St Levan church (near the end of point 5).

1 From the seaward end of the car park, take the path signed Porthcurno Beach and Coast Path. (For a note on Porthcurno, see pages 20-21.) **Where the path splits into three, join the coastal footpath heading west by following the narrow one, more-or-less straight ahead.** As it winds gently uphill it gives fine views of the beach and Treryn Dinas headland, famous for its Logan Rock (see pages 23-24, and the photograph on page 38).

Soon you reach a choice of ways to the top of the cliff. If you continue ahead you have a long flight of steps to climb, but that is probably easier than the alternative, a zigzag path which is very steep in places. Both routes eventually bring you to the entrance to the Minack Theatre car park, and from there the coast path is clearly signed, via a kissing gate on the right.

THE MINACK THEATRE

Rowena Cade was born in 1893, the daughter of a wealthy mill owner. With her mother she moved to Porthcurno, which had been a favourite holiday venue, in 1923, following her father's death. They had built a house on the clifftop and named it Minack House, since it stood above Minack ("stony") Point. Rowena was not an actress, but enjoyed making costumes and sets for amateur theatricals; hence, in 1929 or '30 she became involved with a local company who were putting on "A Midsummer Night's Dream" in a wooded meadow nearby. They planned to present "The Tempest" next, and wanted a clifftop setting for it. The garden at Minack House looked ideal, except that there was no room for an audience; but Miss Cade was undaunted, and decided to build a terrace at the bottom of the garden for a stage, using the granite outcrops on either side as "wings" and the curved slope above for a few rows of tiered sets. With the help of just two men she carried out this huge task, involving moving masses of earth and granite boulders, during the winter of 1931-2. (A vivid description of this feat is given by Averil Demuth in "The Minack Open-Air Theatre", published by David & Charles in 1968.)

In August 1932 "The Tempest" was performed on the grassy terrace, with lighting supplied mainly by batteries and car headlights - plus "an obliging moon"! 1933 saw a production of "Twelfth Night" in which two professional actors joined the local players, and then a play was presented in alternate years until the outbreak of war. During the war the theatre was used as the set for several scenes in a film, "Love Story", starring Margaret Lockwood and Stewart Grainger; but so much damage was done by the army and Italian prisoners of war that Miss Cade and her two men had to start almost from scratch to prepare for the first post-war production, Euripides' "Trojan Women" performed by pupils of Penzance grammar schools in 1949. A "pill-box" left over from the war made an ideal box office!

Huge expansion and many improvements to the theatre have taken place since then, and the annual programme consists now of as many as 17 productions. Rowena Cade was often to be seen taking her place to watch the plays in the old wheelbarrow which had shifted so many tons of rock, sand and earth. She died aged 89 in 1983, and her tireless work and enthusiasm are commemorated in a special Exhibition Centre.

Brochures giving details of the current season's performances are widely available; information about the programme and the Visitor Centre (open daily 9.30-5.30 except during matinees) can be obtained by phoning 01736 810181 or visiting the website, www.minack.com.

At several points from here on you will have to decide between inland paths - often easier and more direct - and cliff-edge alternatives with better views. The latter are usually somewhat narrower and less well defined, may involve some mild scrambling, and in a few cases are strictly for those with a good head for heights; but the first example, a short path leading to the National Trust headland, Pedn-men-an-mere, presents no such problems.

PEDN-MEN-AN-MERE

The old Cornish language name means "the great stone headland", but about a century ago this place acquired an English nickname, Wireless Point. In

1902 a tall radio mast was erected here, and the means by which it was anchored to the ground and supported by cables are still clear to see. *People at first called it the Marconi Mast, thinking it was part of the wireless telegraphy operation based at Poldhu, on the Lizard peninsula (it even appeared on the contemporary Ordnance Survey 6-inch map as "Marconi Signal Station Pole"), but in fact it was the property*

of a rival body, the Eastern Telegraph Company, and its purpose was to "spy" on Marconi's transatlantic signals. The mast was taken down in 1914 on the orders of the War Office. Des Hannigan, in his National Trust "Coast of Cornwall" leaflet (No.11 in the series) refers to the "exquisite irony" of this, since the reason given was that it could be misused for purposes of espionage! For much more detail, see J.E.Packer's booklet, "The Spies at Wireless Point".

Back on the coast path, you next descend almost the whole way to Porth Chapel beach, and then as you start climbing again you soon come to the remains of St Levan's Holy Well.

ST LEVAN'S CHAPEL & WELL

J.T.Blight visited this place in about 1870 and wrote, "This was the spot chosen by St Levan for his chapel or hermitage, which stood on the verge of the cliff; the well was farther back, but steps communicated from one to the other; these, however, have disappeared. The site of the chapel can only be guessed at, whilst the walls of the little baptistery are widely overgrown by rushes and water plants. Thus is the altar overthrown, the shrine deserted, and the holy place become a wilderness." ("A Week at the Land's End") Since then, however, the vegetation around the well has been cleared, the granite blocks of the little building beside it have been repointed, and the remains of about fifty steps down to the ruins of the chapel - on a ledge against the cliff - were revealed in an excavation during the 1930s.

St Levan (more accurately, St Selevan) was of royal stock. He is said to have been born at Bosliven, about half a mile south-east of St Buryan, during the 6th century, and to have lived at Bodellan, at the northern edge of what is now Porthcurno. One of the many legends about him is briefly told in the later note about St Levan church; for the rest, see J.C.Burr's book, usually on sale in the church.

Above the well, the coast path continues to the left, up more steps. At the top you have a good view of St Levan church, which will be visited towards the end of the walk. In the distance ahead now can be seen the Gwennap Head coastguard lookout and the spire-like rock formation atop Chairladder Cliff near Hella, which Blight calls "the Fairies' Point". (Chairladder - much frequented by rock climbers - may have derived its name from the old legend of a male witch called Harry an Lader, "Harry the thief", who occupied it as his "break-neck chair" while he conjured up storms. Another storm-raising witch, Madge Figgy, is said to have operated from the same place: one story tells of a ship she destroyed by luring it into Porth Loe. The tales of Madge or Madgy Figgy are told in vivid detail by Robert Hunt in his *Popular Romances of the West of England*, 1881.) Closer at hand, the granite has everywhere been weathered into fascinating shapes, often resembling human or animal forms.

Next the path descends, amongst huge granite boulders at first, then between tall garden hedges, to the narrow cove of Porthgwarra.

PORTHGWARRA

The name of this tiny fishing village may mean "harbour at the wooded slope" or simply "higher cove", but in 16th-century documents it appears as Porth Cluythen or Porth Kilwethan, "hazel-tree cove".

The tunnel down to the beach (shown here) is man-made, the work of miners from St Just: it enabled farmers to fetch seaweed as fertiliser, and possibly also sand to help neutralise the acid soil. (See the later note about Nanjizal.) If you go down through it you will see a smaller  *tunnel leading seawards (shown on the opposite page); this, to quote from John Chappell's Points of Interest leaflet (usually available in the tea-room)*

"was the fishermen's access to the tidal 'hulleys' built in the rocks to store shellfish. The 'hulleys', which are no longer used, had wooden floors and top covers with trapdoors." Michael Williams refers to them as "wells", used to keep crabs and crayfish alive. At the top of the steep, rough slipway is a winch, and to the left of that as you face inland used to stand a large wooden capstan; it was dismantled in the 1950s according to the lady who runs the tearoom. The cavities in the rock behind *"are said to have been used as pigs' houses"* writes Mr Chappell.

Looking seawards from the top of the slip - perhaps from the comfort of the seat there - notice the masses of bromeliads growing on the left - dark-green, spiky leaves, often tinged deep red - and further away a great bank of perennial mesembryanthemum *("Sally-my-Handsome"* in Cornwall!), otherwise called ice plants or hottentot figs. They speak of mild winters here, despite the often fierce westerly gales that make life hard and dangerous for fishermen.

The death at sea of a Porthgwarra fisherman occurs in the sad story of William and Nancy, which ends with the deranged girl stepping into the waves beside the ghost of her lover. Porthgwarra *"was once known as Sweethearts' Cove"*, say Tony Deane and Tony Shaw.

2 **From Porthgwarra you could return to Porthcurno via St Levan church by following the directions at the end of the introductory note.**

Continuing westwards on the coast path, you soon have the option of forking left on a narrower path out towards Gwennap Head, from which it runs on at quite a low level before rejoining the main coast path. Don't risk it if you have no head for heights, but it does provide fine views, in particular of a huge blow-hole, caused by the collapse of clifftop rock into a sea cave. It is this which gives Gwennap Head its Cornish name, Tol-Pedn-Penwith, "Penwith's holed headland".

If you keep to the main path, you will pass just seawards of the two landmark cones and the Gwennap Head coastguard lookout.

WALK 3

THE RUNNELSTONE

The black-and-white and red landmarks are so placed as to line up with the position of the Runnelstone, a submerged rock at the far end of a long reef, about three-quarters of a mile offshore. The rock used to show above surface as a tiny island about 4 metres long by 2 wide, and in 1855, following three shipwrecks on it the previous year, Trinity House erected an iron beacon plus mast on it, but storms washed all that away only a year later. Finally, on 8th October 1923, the steamer "City of Westminster" knocked off the top of the rock; its position, twenty feet below the surface now, is marked these days by a buoy which flashes at night, and on all but the very calmest of days rings a bell and emits the mournful note which you have probably been hearing for some time. "Moaning Minnie", the locals call it, says Mr Packer (see Further Reading), and he gives a detailed explanation of how the "sort of giant organ pipe" works. The story of the wreck of the "City of Westminster" is told by Richard Larn and Clive Carter.

From the high ground here the view ahead now extends to Land's End, with the Wolf Rock lighthouse on its island about eight miles to the southwest of Land's End, and Sennen church tower on the skyline. The path now descends to a wooden footbridge over marshy ground not far above the level of the boulder beach of Porth Loe cove (noted in the annals of maritime history for the wreck of the full-rigged iron ship, the *Khyber*, in March 1905, when only three of the crew of 26 survived). It then climbs again to give good views of the next promontory, Carn Barra. The name means "carn of the loaf", referring apparently to the shape of the granite boulders on the clifftop; *Murray's Handbook* of 1859 mentions "other freaks of form" such as "on the profile of the cliff, the figure of a lady at her devotions". Beyond that is the largest of the coves so far seen - so large, it seems, that it comes in the plural: Pendower ("head of the water") Coves. It is / they are easily recognisable from the huge sea cave at the far end and the rocky Bosistow Island - the home of thousands of seabirds - close to the northern headland, Carn Les Boel. This name is explained by Craig Weatherhill as "ruined fort at an axe-shaped outcrop", referring, he says, to the Iron Age cliff castle there. (It has not been excavated, and remains of it are scanty, but there are ramparts and a ditch on the north side of the headland, parts of another rampart across the neck, and two large boulders which may have formed jambs of the gateway.)

The path skirts, on the landward side, a large mound of granite boulders, and then comes your first view of an even larger cove than Pendower - large enough, in fact, to be called a bay. This is Mill Bay, otherwise Nanjizal ("low valley"). The path descends quite steeply, joining a wide bridleway shortly before crossing the stream via a footbridge.

NANJIZAL

The spelling in Murray's 1859 Handbook, "Nanjissel", shows how the word is pronounced. The anonymous author calls it "a wild, romantic scene", and refers to "the ruins of the mill" by the shore. All that's left of the mill now is the impressive granite wheelpit, just inland from the footbridge. It is usually assumed to have been a corn mill, probably belonging to Higher Bosistow farm, which is linked to it by the bridleway just mentioned, but Michael Williams in his book "Around Land's End" mentions that some researchers believe the wheel operated tin stamps. "The valley down which the stream runs from Polgigga," he says, "has been known to generations of local people as Stamps Bottoms and a farm there, is named Stamps Farm." St Levan parish is usually said to have been one of the very few in Cornwall to have no history of mining, but the 1859 Handbook refers to prospecting pits near the cliff edge on the southern side, and "a picturesque crane" which stood on the opposite side, lifting sand from the beach. Whether this was in pursuit of detrital tin or for agricultural use the author does not say, but the latter seems more likely, because the sand is lime-rich, consisting mainly of broken shells.

It is worth descending the wooden staircase to the beach. The steps are a recent improvement: scrambling down and up was always part of the Nanjizal experience. The sand is sometimes swept away to leave only boulders like those at Porth Loe. (One of the impossible tasks said to have been given to the "doomed spirit" of Tregeagle was to sweep the sand of Porthcurno beach to Nanjizal, only for the Gulf Stream to sweep it back.) The great cleft in the cliff on the left through which the water surges (photo overleaf) has been called "The Song of the Sea"; another name is Zawn Pyg, "Bird's Beak Cave": "Taking the cave for the eye, and the tongue of rock for the beak, the resemblance to a bird's head is obvious," claims our Handbook writer. On the other side of the stream, which reaches the beach as a small waterfall, is a deep cave.

3 **To start the inland walk back to Porthcurno, retrace your steps for a few yards, then continue up the wide bridleway mentioned above. Keep left at the junction with another bridleway, and you soon reach the buildings of Higher Bosistow farm.**

Nanjizal beach from the coast path

4 **Turn right, following the red arrow, and just after the left bend cross the rather narrow stone stile on the right, where there are two wooden posts, each bearing a yellow arrow. Ignore the path going to the right: the one you want runs almost straight ahead, close to a low wall on your left. Follow the wall where it turns left and cross the next stile. The path now goes diagonally to the left across a fairly large field to another stile beside a farm gate at the far corner; now continue in the same line towards the buildings of Arden Sawah farm. There is a stile a few yards to the left of the farm gate.** The intriguing farm name appears to mean "silver stream"; perhaps it refers to the stream at the foot of Ardensawah Cliff, which overlooks Pendower Coves.

5 **Turn left on the metalled lane, then sharp-right at the road, signposted to Porthgwarra. Ignore the signed public footpath on the left at the right-hand bend, but take the one, also on the left, about a hundred metres further on. St Levan church tower can be seen now, and the path heads more-or-less directly towards it all the way, crossing a series of the granite cattle-grids known as "Cornish stiles". At one of them, as you approach the church, another path is signed to the right.** A small Celtic cross stands at the junction of the paths. It is so eroded as to be scarcely recognisable, but you will find it among the granite stones on your right after crossing the stile. **Continue ahead with the hedge on your left at first; after about 50 metres cross the stile in the hedge, and walk on down. After one more stile you pass beside a pair of cottages and enter the churchyard.**

ST LEVAN CHURCH

It dates mainly from the 15th century, and was restored in 1876, but some parts of the 12th-century building remain. It is unusually well supplied with guide books and leaflets, so I need do no more than point out the most striking features. Inside, notice the Norman font, and especially the beautiful carved bench-ends, both old and new. They are very fully described and illustrated in Jeffery C. Burr's history. The Lady Chapel, at the south-eastern end of the church, was added late in the 1920s.

Outside, the 18th-century sundial above the entrance to the south porch bears a Latin inscription meaning "The days pass like shadows." In the churchyard are several interesting graves, including that of William Bottrell (1816-81), a pioneer in the recording of Cornish myths and legends. Many other graves are of shipwreck victims, the best known of which is that of Richard Wetherall, captain of the brig "Aurora" which sank in 1811. He is said to have sounded eight bells as the ship went down, and now if you hear eight bells sounding from his grave you will die within the year. Elsewhere there is the communal grave of 23 who died when the "Khyber" was wrecked in 1905.

The St Levan Stone, a large granite boulder split in two, is on your left as you leave the church. In early times it was associated with fertility rites, and it is said that the Christian cross was set beside it in order to "neutralise" the pagan element. Legend tells that as St Levan sat on the stone he cracked it open with his staff and spoke the following rhyme:

When with panniers astride
A pack horse can ride
Through St Levan's Stone
The world will be done.

Another version of the story attributes the prophecy to Merlin. According to one account the gap is now considerably wider than it was in the 17th century, but Robert Hunt gave the reassuring news that he could detect no difference over a period of fifty years. The ornamented cross, seven feet tall, is desribed by Arthur Langdon (1896) as "one of the most elegant and well-proportioned wheel crosses to be found throughout Cornwall."

6 **Leave the churchyard at the north-east corner, starting at the impressive "coffin stile", a wide flight of steps with a coffin-shaped stone at the top.** The path ahead is known as the Coffin Path: those carrying the deceased from Porthcurno would rest the coffin on the slab here, to be met by the priest before descending to the church. Once there was an ancient Celtic cross at each of the six entrances to the churchyard; the simple wheel cross on the right here is the only one surviving intact. A rectangular fragment of another cross, showing a crucifix figure, is built into the hedge on the left. **After a small wooden gate, the path crosses a fairly large field, passing another old Celtic cross on the left.** The simple, unornamented wheel cross is described by Arthur Langdon as "massive and rudely executed"; the granite is exceptionally coarse.

7 **On reaching Rospletha farm buildings, turn right on the lane, continue down to the Mariners Lodge Hotel, and turn left down the main road to return to the Porthcurno car park.** Take care here: traffic can be quite heavy, especially in the summer.

Treryn Dinas from Porthcurno Beach   *(Photograph by Stephanie Acton)*

WALK 4
SENNEN COVE, LAND'S END & NANJIZAL
About 5 miles; or it could be done as two walks of about 3 miles each.

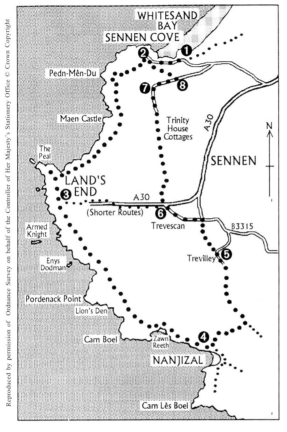

The cliff scenery and the long views you can enjoy on this walk are wonderful, and the places seen are full of historical interest. This section of the South West Way (coast path) is mostly in very good condition, and the slightly gravelly nature of the earth makes it unlikely to be slippery even in wet weather. The main path in general stays well away from precipitous drops, and even the narrower side-paths which offer better views are unlikely to worry those nervous about heights. I need, though, to warn you that along a fairly short stretch as you approach Nanjizal the path does run close to the edge - uncomfortably close, for some people, especially in windy weather. This part of the route is then followed by the only lengthy steep climb, as the walk turns inland. I hope you won't be deterred by these remarks - just prepared!

Refreshments and toilets are available at both Sennen Cove and Land's End: food is available all year round at the Longships Family Restaurant & Bar, attached to the Land's End Hotel, and at the Old Success Inn at Sennen Cove. (The Inn takes its name from one of the seine net companies which used to fish for pilchards here; the company used to pay out its profits in the bar.) The shops, cafés and toilets at the Cove, and the

39

Smugglers Burger Bar, Pasty Shop and Cornish Pantry at Land's End, are closed in winter.

The suggested start/end point for this walk is Sennen Cove, which has two car parks, both of which charge £2.50 for a stay long enough to complete this walk (2003 prices, applicable all year round). At the height of the summer season you would be well advised to get there early in order to find a space. In the winter, roadside parking in the village is permitted, but please make sure not to impede access for other vehicles. Directions are given from the large car park on the right as you reach the foot of the hill; if you use the Harbour Car Park, at the far end of the village, pick up the directions at point 2.

You could equally well base the complete walk on the Land's End car park (£3.00 per car for all-day parking, again in 2003); this would also give you the option of roughly halving the length of the walk by omitting Sennen Cove. For this, pick up the directions at point 3.

1 Walk along the seafront road, passing the Old Success, and later the lifeboat house (the largest in Britain and well worth a visit) and the Roundhouse where the big capstan was originally housed; it is now a craft centre. Down to the right is the harbour.

SENNEN COVE

The word "cove" is there only to distinguish it from the Churchtown above. John Corin and others who have written about its history call it a fishing station rather than a fishing cove. There is no natural harbour. Kings (Athelstan, Stephen and John) and a would-be king (Perkin Warbeck) all landed here, as did Danish and Spanish invaders, but all would have had to do what the fishermen did till quite recent times: dodge the many submerged or half-submerged rocks and islets scattered across Whitesand Bay and pull up their boats on to the beach.

Eventually - nobody seems to know exactly when - a rudimentary harbour was created by clearing boulders away from a channel at the southern end of the beach, cutting back part of the cliff there, and using flat granite stones to build a slipway (known still as The Caunse, from the Cornish word for a paved or cobbled way) with a large capstan at the top. The round building housing the capstan had a loft and conical roof added to it in 1886. The Caunse was given protection on the western side by a drystone wall about twenty feet tall, The Wharf. This last is said

to have been built in the early 1870s by the men employed to construct the second Longships lighthouse, during periods when weather conditions kept them on the mainland. A thatch-roofed "pilchard palace", called The Press, was built on top of The Wharf; this was demolished soon after World War I, making way for what is now the Harbour Car Park. The huge annual harvest of pilchards which sustained the seine-fishing companies ceased early in the 20th century; what continues today is mainly crabbing and the catching of mackerel and mullet.

John Corin's book is well worth seeking out if you are interested in the history of the lifeboat service at Sennen: the fascination lies in the drama and the detail, and I have room for neither here. Sennen's first lifeboat, less than 26 feet long and propelled by six oars, arrived in 1853. The problems involved in launching her and her 10-oar successors were daunting: mounted on a carriage, the boat had to be drawn by a team of eight horses from the lifeboat house along the road and down the beach, then manhandled into the water - tough work even in calm conditions, impossible sometimes in stormy weather. On one occasion the boat had to be taken overland for launching at Penberth. Use of Sennen's granite slip for launching was only a partial success. When the "Khyber" was wrecked at Porth Loe in 1905 the Sennen boat was unable to put to sea, and as a result at long last an adequate breakwater was provided. In 1919 a railway slip was built, in preparation for the arrival of Sennen's first motor lifeboat, but still there were problems with launching: a much longer and steeper slip was needed, and this was completed by 1929, together with a second, shorter slip for rehousing and a large enough *boathouse to accommodate a turntable. Today Sennen has a 47-foot Tyne-class All-Weather Lifeboat, the "Norman Salvesen", capable of 18 knots, and a faster inshore boat, "Spirit of the A.C.C." A team of 24 volunteers is available, so that both boats can be manned at all times.*

2 From the Harbour Car Park, take the uphill path. Soon you come to a flight of steps, where an acorn sign on a wooden post confirms that you are on the coast path. The large building high above was the Sennen Cove Hotel. **After the right turn, take the stony path up to what looks like a miniature castle keep.** (The lower path comes to a dead end, but you may want to divert briefly along it for the magnificent view. It was from here, or close by, that the huer would keep watch for shoals of pilchards and mullet, and on sighting them would shout "Hevva!", meaning "flocking, shoaling", and direct the shooting of a seine with a pair of black canvas globes known as "bushes".) The "keep" is actually a former coastguard lookout, now owned by the National Trust; details of its history are given on the building. The concrete base just below is a relic of World War 2. The headland above which you now are is Pedn-men-du, meaning "black-rock head"; the prominent rock just south of it is known as the Irish Lady. Some say that from the correct angle it resembles a lady in a long cloak; others aver that an Irish ship was wrecked here, the only survivor being a beautiful lady who clung to the rock.

Continue along the coast path. Not far from the lookout, the fairly slight remains of two Bronze Age round barrows lie close to the main path. The slightly narrower side-paths on the right are worth exploring. In December 2003 some of the early ones, on Mayon Cliff, gave excellent views of what remained of the RMS *Mulheim*.

THE WRECK OF THE "MULHEIM"

The "Mulheim", en route from Cork to Lübeck, was driven ashore at Castle Zawn in the early hours of the morning on 22 March 2003. A helicopter from RNAS Culdrose lifted off the crew. The vessel featured in national and local news coverage for many weeks afterwards because of her cargo, 2,200 tonnes of waste non-biodegradable plastic, thought by experts to be a danger to marine wildlife. Despite much bad weather, the salvage operation had successfully removed the bulk of the plastic when the wreck had to be finally abandoned at the end of May, by which time all her decks were split. She broke in two on 7th October.

The "Mulheim" photographed in December 2003

Castle Zawn ("zawn" meaning cleft or chasm) takes its name from a nearby Iron Age fortification, Maen Castle ("maen", stone - "Mayon" is another version of it), easily visited by taking another side-path. About 30 yards beyond the National Trust "Maen Cliff Castle" sign, you pass through the narrow gateway in the defensive wall and on to the small headland. Archaeologists have concluded that the fortification dates from before 300 BC; if they are right, this is the oldest of such structures in Cornwall. Its inhabitants are presumed to have built the stone boundary walls of the fields on the hillslope above. Not far beyond this, several tiny streams cross the coast path, no doubt once a crucial fresh-water supply for the cliff-castle dwellers.

Further south, much of the surrounding clifftop was, late in 2003, fenced off because it had recently been re-seeded, and one of the cliff-edge paths was temporarily closed because of subsidence; it should have been reopened by the time this book is published.

WALK 4
LAND'S END

"This Holy Place of Tourisme" was J.R.A.Hockin's phrase for it in the 1930s. Nearly 200 years earlier, when John Wesley first saw it, he described it as "an awful sight"; in his day, "awful" meant awe-inspiring, but there are many people today - especially Cornish people - who would accept Wesley's words in the modern sense. They have in mind, of course, not the natural scenery but what man has done to it.

The creation of what we see now at Land's End began in 1982, when it was sold - not to the National Trust, as many had hoped, but to a Welshman, David Goldstone, for £2¼ million. His company set up exhibitions and other visitor attractions and introduced an admission charge. This was greeted with outrage by those who saw it merely as an exercise in commercial exploitation of the jewel in the crown of Cornwall's natural heritage. Many were sceptical when told that the need to raise money was essentially in order to finance a major conservation programme. If they were honest, though, they couldn't deny that the clifftop area at Land's End had been neglected for decades: it was littered with tatty, semi-derelict buildings and suffering severely from erosion. The conservation programme involved improved drainage and such anti-erosion measures as the building of a railway down to the "First and Last House" in order to protect the turf from trampling feet. After Peter de Savary bought the site in 1987, major additions to the "theme park" were made (for example. the "Last Labyrinth" came in 1988), and the conservation projects intensified, overseen by leading botanists, notably David Bellamy. This work continued under later owners, and there were certainly plenty of signs that it was still ongoing during the winter of 2003-4. The "First and Last Farm" at Greeb and the Wildlife Discovery Centre run by the RSPB also enhance the modern Land's End's environmentally-friendly image.

In the August 1993 issue of "An Baner Kernewek" ("The Cornish Banner") magazine, Jeremy Jacobson and Annabel Barber wrote: "Think of Land's End and Tintagel, to name but two once lovely, now monstrous places. Why do these people have to come with their petty, mean values, foisting them on a land they do not understand and never will, and that will vanish without trace if something is not done to contain their rapacity?" Two years later, Land's End was highly commended in a publication called "Operation Excellence", and praised in these words: "It has been developed with a sensitivity which is quite remarkable when you compare it with places like Blackpool." What do you think?

WALK 4

As you approach the cluster of modern buildings constituting the Land's End theme park, there is a choice of ways. The most interesting is down to the right, where the "First and Last Refreshment House in England" stands, above The Peal, the westernmost point of mainland Britain. (An unromantic name for a place of such fame, deriving probably from a Cornish word meaning pile or heap, or a Breton one meaning simply rock.) 1¼ miles from it is the Longships Lighthouse; more than 8 miles away, and visible only in very clear conditions, is Wolf Rock Lighthouse.

THE LAND'S END LIGHTHOUSES

Built between 1870 and 1873 to replace a much smaller one completed in 1795, the Longships Lighthouse stands on one of a group of small islands which are said to resemble a fleet of Viking longships. In the days before radio and telephones, the keepers used semaphore to communicate with their wives in Trinity House Cottages, which stand above Sennen Cove. (You will pass them near the end of this walk.) Like all other British lighthouses, it is now fully automated.

Wolf Rock has "engulfed" many an unfortunate ship (hence the name, probably: old maps name it "Gulf" or "Gulph"). The lighthouse there was built between 1862 and 1869: fascinating details about the skill and courage involved in its construction are given by Michael Tarrant in "Cornwall's Lighthouse Heritage". In 1976 it became the first lighthouse in the world to be equipped with a helicopter landing platform above the light.

Close to The Peal is the rock known as Dr Syntax's Head. Dr Syntax was a fictitious clergyman invented by a very minor poet, William Coombe, and depicted in a series of comic pictures by Thomas Rowlandson between 1812 and 1823. The weathered granite boulder which is supposed to resemble his features is well shown in a photo in Michael Williams's books, *Around Land's End* and *Around & About Land's End*. The "First and Last House" is said to have some features typical of 17th-century buildings; it probably originated as, or stands on the site of, a shepherd's hut. Already by the 1860s a lady from Sennen was providing refreshments for visitors in it. **From there, walk over (or beside, if you don't fancy it) the swaying suspension bridge across Dollar Cove.** The name suggests coins salvaged from a wreck, or perhaps even the grief

45

("dolour") of those bereaved, but is more likely to derive from the Breton word *talar*, which could refer to a pointed rock or sea-stack. **Continue past the RSPB Wildlife Discovery building and the little round hut where for a fiver (2003) you can have your photo taken beside the famous Land's End signpost.** A rock below this is Dr Johnson's Head, because it looks like the "Great Cham," complete with wig.

3 Unless you want to visit the various "attractions" (I can vouch for the quality of the pasties, and people tell me the Last Labyrinth is brilliant), **EITHER return to Sennen Cove. For the inland route, walk through the theme-park complex and along the footpath on the left side of the vehicular access road. When this becomes the A30 there is a pavement on the right.   Eventually you will come to the junction with the B3315 road (to Porthcurno and St Buryan).   Here take the signed public footpath on the left, and pick up the directions at point 6.**

OR continue along the coast path, which at first runs beside the wall on the seaward side of the Land's End Hotel and soon afterwards crosses a wooden footbridge.   The official path, now heading south-east, mostly stays quite well inland, but once again there are narrower paths off to the right which give you breathtaking views of Greeb Zawn (which takes its name from Carn Greeb, "crest crag", which in turn gives its name to "The Land of Greeb Farm and Crafts", down to the left); the island known, for no obvious reason (but ingenious theories abound), as the Armed Knight; the boulder-covered beach beside the holed Enys Dodnan ("enys" meaning island, but it's an island only at high tide); and the impressive Pordenack Point headland, where the jointing in the granite (caused by contraction as the magma - molten rock - cooled) creates

what is known as "castellated" cliffs. "All the wild grandeur of the Land's End coast seems to be focussed on this great stack of granite blocks," wrote J.R.A. Hockin. The name,

Looking across the boulder beach to Pordenack Point

*Picnic stop with a view of Enys Dodnan, the Armed Knight,
and the Land's End complex*

Pordenack, includes the Cornish "dyn", meaning fort; it would indeed be surprising if it had not been fortified in Iron Age times. Not far past that, as you approach the equally majestic Carn Boel (possibly "bare crag") promontory, you are walking on Trevilley Cliff, above Zawn Trevilley, with its great cave called the Lion's Den. Here the eroded granite forms are truly amazing: almost everything invites photography. Steps down to a fairly stagnant little stream above a gully, then steeply up, soon bring you to another side-path which leads out on to Carn Boel, and now you have your first view of Nanjizal (or Mill) Bay.

A short length of fence on the right marks the point where the path runs above Zawn Reeth (Cornish, "red chasm"; photo, page 48). Here the little beach is divided by a pinnacle of granite known as the Diamond Horse, a name which refers to diamond-like quartz crystals in the rock. Zawn Reeth has its place in history: in October 1869 it became the first location in Cornwall where a submarine telegraph cable was brought ashore. The plan was to link the mainland with Scilly. Unfortunately, it seems that the cable-laying steamer, the *Fuselier*, went badly off-course on its trip to the islands, so that the end of the cable was reached before it

Zawn Reeth and the Diamond Horse, with Nanjizal Bay beyond

got there! The story of how the engineer in charge at St Mary's nevertheless managed to give the impression that he was duly receiving signals from Nanjizal is told by J.E.Packer in *Messages under the Sea*.

As you walk on you may notice a few small features on your left, such as a fairly deep cave and what looks like a small quarry, evidence of prospecting by miners. The note about Nanjizal on page 35 refers to this topic.

As mentioned in the introduction to this walk, the path on this side of the bay runs, perhaps alarmingly, close to the cliff edge in two or three places; do please tread with special care.

4 You will still be quite a way above the beach when you come to the inland path you need to take to return to your start-point; it is clearly indicated below the coast-path sign on a wooden post. (Of course, it's well worth going on down to the beach area first.) **Here is the very steep climb I warned you about - quite a scramble in places - and once you're up to the level area above you may find the path rather overgrown with gorse and brambles.** Ahead now you can see St Buryan church tower on the skyline. **Ignore the path on the right, heading down into the valley. After the kissing gate, continue straight ahead across a field.** Now you can see Sennen church. **Past a metal farm gate, the path heads slightly to the left; next, an open gateway, and the path crosses the field beyond; then another gate with a rather awkward-looking stile on its left; and finally you are on the rather rough lane which runs beside the group of houses and farm buildings at Trevilley.** Early owners of the Trevilley estate were a family named Vingoe, said to be of Norman descent. Legend tells that the approaching death of a Vingoe was always marked by "chains of fire ascending and descending" on Trevilley Cliff, "often accompanied by loud and frightful noises. It is said that these tokens have not been seen since the last male of the family came to a violent end." (The quotation is from Robert Hunt, who also mentions the tradition that the estate took its name from "the ancient counts of Treville" in France, but Cornish "Beli's farm" is much more likely.)

5 Where the lane bends right, cross the stile ahead, go through the wooden gate and continue ahead beside the farmhouse to another stile on the right of a farm gate. Luckily it's not too difficult to avoid splashing through the mud churned up by the cattle on the far side. As you walk on, watch out for the interesting old wayside cross placed just the other side of the hedge on your right - just past the point where the hedge takes a little side-step. It is round-headed but the side you can see has a latin cross with the figure of Christ carved on it. As Andrew Langdon points out, its position here reflects the fact that you are on an ancient path linking Sennen and St Levan churches. **Another stile at the corner, and the path goes on in the same line to a metal kissing gate in front of a further stile. The entrance drive to the house on your right now brings you to a road; turn left on that. This is the B3315, which can be moderately busy in summer; even at other times it's best to walk on the right side.** There are several interesting old houses along here, such as "Vingoe Cottage" (see the earlier remarks about Trevilley), and another house on the left beside which an old cottage has been partially demolished, leaving a large fireplace with cloam oven on the left side. The Land's End Trekking Centre is the explanation for the large number of horses you are likely to see hereabouts.

Since this walk does not pass through the main part of Sennen Churchtown, I'll resist the temptation to include a note about it. Suffice it to say (1) that most things there [pubs, shops, garages ...] are "the first and last" of their kind; (2) that little or nothing is known about St Sennen or Senan; and (3) that the little parish church is well worth a visit. The Church Guide booklet usually available there is both interesting and entertaining.

6 **At the T-junction, cross the A30 with due care and take the signed footpath straight ahead, keeping to the right of the house. A little footbridge is followed by a stone stile. Now ignore the narrow path that keeps near the left edge of the field; take the more obvious one, further right, which eventually brings you to a metal kissing-gate. From there, continue ahead, through an open gateway (or over the stile on the right side), and now head for the large white building ahead, which is in fact Trinity House (coastguard) Cottages. Beyond a wooden stile and stream, the path runs beside the wall surrounding the cottages, and finally what was, late in 2003, an extremely dilapidated wooden kissing-gate admits you to a surfaced lane. This soon becomes a minor road.**

7 **Keep to the road as it bends right. You continue along here for nearly a quarter of a mile.**

8 **Don't miss the path down on your left, signposted to Sennen Cove; it starts at a point opposite the drive to a very pretty thatched cottage.** The seat nearly half-way down gives a wonderful view across Whitesand Bay, the long stretch of dunes created by the prevailing south-west winds blowing beach-sand as much as nearly half a mile inland, and further along the coast to Cape Cornwall; and of the nearby slate reefs, visible as islets with intriguing names such as Cowloe, Bo Cowloe and Little Bo. **The path eventually becomes Stone Chair Lane** (another intriguing name; some day soon, no doubt, a kind reader will explain it to me), **and brings you down to the Roundhouse beside the Harbour Car Park.**

WALK 5
ST JUST AND THE NANQUIDNO AND COT VALLEYS
Nearly five miles

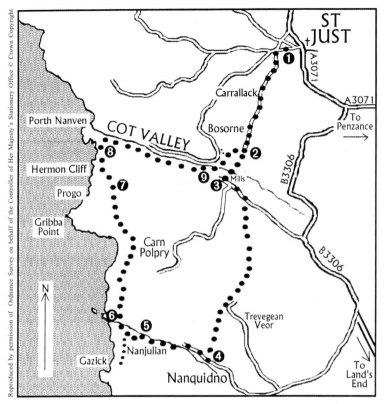

This is a walk amidst delightful scenery, including a fine stretch of cliffs and two very contrasting valleys, one of which (Nanquidno) is probably the prettiest of all the valleys that run down to the coast in St Just parish. Its alternative name, Nanjulian, could be translated as "valley nook", which seems apt. There are few surviving mine buildings on this route, but the evidence of early mining activity is equally interesting if you know how to recognise it.

There are some rather steep climbs on the coast here, and the field paths are likely to be muddy, but in general the stiles are well maintained. Shops, pubs and toilets are available only in St Just.

Des Hannigan's *Wildlife Walkabouts* book, if you can find a copy, would be a useful companion, because it has a detailed account of the flora and fauna to be seen in the Cot Valley and on the high ground to the south.

WALK 5
ST JUST

"We came to St Just," wrote W.G.Maton in the 1790s, "a sad, dreary place, situated in a most inhospitable and cheerless corner of the county." A century later,"Edward Bosanketh" described it as "large, yet unattractive. ... The houses are scattered about over a large area; and in one place, where they are sufficiently numerous to form two or three streets, the collection has been dignified by the name of 'town', though the reason is no clearer than why a triangular piece of ground in the centre should be called the 'square'." This was more than matched by the Edwardian guidebook quoted by Gerald Priestland: "a dreary town that has seen better days, smug, commonplace ... without a trace of beauty or interest ..." John Betjeman gave a more balanced view: "It is too workaday a place to be likely to be turned into a self-conscious tourist resort" - and that, of course, is part of its charm.

The parish's growth from a small, predominantly agricultural community of under 3,000 in 1800 to a mainly industrial populace of 9,000 in 1870, and the decline to some 4,000 in the 1960s, have of course been directly related to the fortunes of its mines - including a china-clay works - and associated enterprises such as Holman's St Just Foundry at Tregeseal. Having its own Mayor (a Mayor, what's more, who's the only one in Britain with a chain of office made of tin), it can indeed be dignified by the name of "town".

Part of St Just churchyard

Churches dominate it - at least three big, impressive nonconformist chapels in addition to the parish church - and pubs to suit all tastes cluster around them. The churchyard, with its two ancient crosses and its gravestones that speak of the harsh realities of life - and death - in a mining parish, is overlooked by some of the most attractive granite cottages in the county. The church itself and the Plen an Gwary are the chief items of "beauty or interest" in the town, and there are separate notes on these in Walks 6 and 7. Although the Market Square / Bank Square area feels like the town centre, Chapel Road rivals it. The biggest Methodist Church is there - which was almost certainly attended by far larger congregations than the parish church, at least in the 19th century, if not still today: John Wesley in 1750 had judged his St Just following to be the biggest in the county, and over a century later "Edward Bosanketh" portrayed the "flock" of the Anglican vicar as being tiny. The primary and secondary schools are close by; so are the Town Hall and the Drill Hall. The latter still bears a plaque showing the symbol of the St Just Battery, whose rifle range was on the cliffs near Kenidjack Head, as mentioned in Walk 7. The town's big annual event, the St Just Feast, starts on the Sunday nearest to 1st November and continues for the following week.

Directions start from the main car park in St Just, which is on Market Street: approaching from the main Penzance road, turn left when you reach the Market Square at the centre of the town, near the church. There are public toilets at the car park.

1 Turn left at the main exit from the car park (opposite the Fire Station and Library on Market Street), and left again at the T-junction. This road, Bosorne Street, takes you past the Methodist Free Church, built in 1860, when the prosperity of the local mines was probably at its height. (As mentioned later, that was also the year in which the Wesleyan Church at St Just was enlarged.) **Continue past the playing field, and where the main lane curves left go on ahead.** There are lots of recent housing developments around here, and more are promised - or threatened, depending on your point of view. The rocky outcrop just beyond the more distant houses up on the left is Carn Bosavern. Carrallack Farm has the sturdy granite buildings typical of this area, and a well on the left which looks as if it's still in at least occasional use. The chicken, ducks and geese in their enclosure, complete with pond, provided lively entertainment when I was last there. Soon you get your first good view, down to the right, of the Cot Valley.

2 Where the track ends, ignore the rough path down on the right. Cross the stile ahead (there is a Public Footpath sign) and take the path that runs straight down towards converted watermill buildings. There were two mills here, Bosavern Mill (the closer of them) and Lower Cot Mill.

There is a second stile to cross and a small wooden gate to go through. As you cross the stream, look right for a good view of the attractive Queen-Anne-period Cot Manor. **After the flight of steps just past Lower Cot Mill you soon come to a minor road.**

3 Turn left on that. Ignore the right turning, but watch for a signed footpath on the left. Don't go that way, but about 15 yards further along take the path on the right, also signed. It starts with some steps up, and continues between hedges - rather brambly here, I'm afraid.

On the left quite close to the stile you come to next is a dump of mine waste, which along with a single shaft are remains of a small mine called Wheal Diamond or possibly Wheal Damsel. It appears to have been active in the 1870s. The building downslope which looks rather like a small engine house is a little reverberatory calciner probably built early last century when some of the dumps were re-worked; beneath the vegetation and rubbish surrounding it are concrete dressing floors.

Continue ahead beside the hedge on your right for a few yards, then go diagonally left across the field to the next stile, of the cattle-grid ("Cornish stile") type. Now go on in the same direction, cutting off the left corner of the field, to stile No. 3. Stile 4 is straight ahead, in the far corner of the next field; stile 5 had a low fence over it. Ahead now on the skyline are Sennen church and Land's End, with the Longships lighthouse out to sea - possibly also, if it's clear enough, the Wolf Rock lighthouse, about 8 miles away, and the Scillies, about 30. Over to the left are two hills, Bartinney Downs and, further south (right), Carn Brea. Not to be confused with the one near Redruth, this is "the last hill in England", at the top of which was a large chamber tomb; that has gone now, however, along with the tiny chapel of St Michael which was built on top of the cairn in the 13th century.

Still continue in the same line, cutting off the left corner and walking by the hedge on the left. The slight remains of stile 6 are on the left of

a gateless gateway, and stile 7 is straight ahead. **Now head just to the right of the cottages at Trevegean. After stile 8 the path runs past them along the left side of the rough, brambly field. Cross stile 9, which has a wooden bar, then keep to the left side of the field, down to an open gateway at the corner. One last stile by a farm gate brings you to a lane that passes Wesley Cottages.** According to an article by R.T.Tonkin, Wesleyan Methodism flourished in Nanquidno from the mid-18th century, and a chapel was built in 1832, at a cost of £60. Over 300 people attended on its opening day; but with the decline in local population as a result of the closure of the mines, eventually "the little edifice stood silent and deserted." It was sold in or soon after 1938, and "is now used as a cowhouse for the adjoining farm." **Beyond farm buildings (perhaps the farm Mr Tonkin referred to) the lane joins the little road running down the Nanquidno Valley.** I have not found an explanation of this name, but it is rather similar to Nanquitho in Sancreed parish, which means "valley of trees".

4 Turn right. Here, at least in winter, among these pretty buildings and the great clumps of bamboo one is surrounded by the sounds of water; but this "sub-tropical" atmosphere lasts only for a few yards, and soon the little valley opens out. Nanjulian Farm makes a pleasing picture, despite the rusty fragments of corrugated-iron roof and the dilapidation of some of the outbuildings. **Beyond the farm, the road declines to a track running beside the stream.** It soon brings you to the farm's corn mill, now converted as a house; the old waterwheel was, we were told, restored in or around the early 1970s. The millpond, now dried out, was up behind the mill, and the course of the leat that fed it is still obvious.

5 Turn left beside the waterwheel, along a path that runs among huge boulders.

Ignore the side-path on the left and go on down towards the sea, where you will find the remains of a mine's dressing

Nanjulian Mill

floors. The most obvious feature is the stone wheelpit. The wheel drove stamps. Nearby are traces (hard to detect now) of buddles and settling tanks, and the revetted banks below the wheelpit may indicate the site of the tin yard. This plant was probably used by Boscregan Mine, one of many small mines in this area of which few if any written records survive. The low heaps of mine waste on the other side of the stream contain water-washed stone, evidence of streamworking.

You might find a short diversion along the coast to the south (left) worthwhile. The coast path starts by ascending a flight of rough steps, at the top of which is an acorn sign. Before long, notice on your left the flooded entrance to an adit, also part of Boscregan Mine. The boulder-strewn "beach" below this, known as the Gazick, was used by a seine fishery during the 19th century. It seems to be a totally unsuitable place to try to land a boat, but there may have been some sand-cover then. Adam Sharpe refers to the ruins of a slipway and several buildings associated with the fishing station, but we didn't find them. Cyril Noall states that "several large iron rings may be seen in the rocks at the north end of the beach to which boats were formerly moored". The seine was apparently defunct by 1880, when the wooden roof of the "Gassac Fish Cellars" was advertised for sale.

6 To continue the round walk, cross the two footbridges at the mouth of the Nanjulian stream. Just beyond the wooden stile (where a National Trust notice refers to the pedigree Longhorn cattle which graze here, thus discouraging gorse and bracken and promoting heather, grass and wildflowers) are signs of mining on and around the cliff-edge, probably relics of a mine called South Levant or Huel Speed. Most obvious is a walled-round shaft. **From here the coast path runs a little way inland up to Carn Polpry.** The name means "claypit", but what claypit there is or was here I don't know. From the top in clear conditions there's a magnificent view. Behind are Sennen church, Sennen Cove and Land's End. Ahead, the islands less than a mile out, sometimes called the Sisters, are officially the Brisons (named from the French word "brisant", breaker, shoal of rocks, reef). Edith Nicholas mentions a local belief that the islands were once used as a prison, and that the name derives from that. She also says they were a favourite picnic spot for young people in Victorian times. The wreck of the brig *New Commercial* on the Brisons in January 1851 is famous because of the outstanding bravery shown by the men who eventually managed to rescue the captain and his wife, stranded on the rocks of Little Brison. Along the coast to the right is Gribba Point, and in the distance Cape Cornwall.

The path descends steeply above Polpry Cove. Another small mine, Wheal Bull, is thought to have been situated here, and if you look back as you near the top of the climb towards Carn Gribba you will see two openings just below the grassy cliff-edge on the far side of the Cove, with a heap of what looks like mine-waste at the foot of the cliff. There are in fact four such openings, according to Adam Sharpe. **At the top of Carn Gribba is a stone stile, and from there the path runs towards Carn Leskys ("burnt tor") and Hermon Cliff, with Progo Cove** (from the Cornish *porth-googoo*, cove of the cave) **below - easily recognisable by the natural arch at its northern end.** Evidence of old mining ventures in the form of shallow pits and trenches is becoming more obvious now. In the 19th century this area was worked by mines called South Wheal Rose, Wheal Oak and Carn-leskis.

HERMON CLIFF

Here the coastline runs roughly at right angles to the direction of the metalliferous lodes, so that they show up particularly clearly in the cliffs. The first attempts were made to follow these deposits inland a very long time ago: Wheal Hermon and the nearby Progo are, Justin Brooke tells me, the first Cornish mines ever to be named on a map (about 1560), and there is no reason to suppose that they were new enterprises then. At the other end of the time-scale, some work was done here as recently as World War I, when Wheal Hermon was still active. There is, however, hardly a trace of any sort of mine building nearby, and certainly no evidence for the use of steam engines: such power as was required for machinery (mainly for hauling ore up to the clifftop) was apparently all provided by horses and the water brought by the leats from the Cot Valley. Hence Adam Sharpe's claim that "there are few stretches of coast in Penwith where the walker is brought face to face with pre-industrial mining technology in quite so dramatic a fashion" as here.

7 **Fork left, downhill, following the coast path acorn sign. A little further down, where the coast path makes a hairpin bend left, you could use the narrower path straight ahead.** Before rejoining the main path this takes you past the first of the remarkable gunnises for which Hermon Cliff is celebrated among students of early metal mining. **The**

narrow path eventually descends to rejoin the main one. You soon pass an awe-inspiring open shaft, then a deep adit on the right, from which a trickle of water runs, followed by three more gunnises, some of them visible down to the left as well as on the right. **It is worth continuing down past more deep cuts to the boulder-strewn beach, known as Church Rock or Nanven Cove,** where the entrance to one mine-working has been surrounded by a massive stone wall.

Sets of what might be taken for bolt-holes in at least two rocks seaward of that are explained by Edith Nicholas when she writes about the Midsummer Eve festivities that took place last century. Miners "would drill a train of holes in a rock, sometimes as many as twenty, and having charged them with black powder, would arrange trails of powder grains from hole to hole, so that as soon as the safety fuse fired the first hole, all succeeding holes would pop in succession." Griff R. Jones's *The Rock Cannon of Gwynnedd* (published by the author in 2002), a detailed study of such "merriment holes", includes a short section about Cornish examples.

To continue the walk, take the low path around the small headland. Notice the way the sea has sculpted the rocks below into soft-looking curves and hollows, like some huge eiderdown; and then on the other side of the point the complex patterns of crisscross lines in the rocks above tide level. **The path soon brings you round to a footbridge over the stream in the Cot Valley**. Beside it are the concrete foundations of a Pelton wheel which was used to drive dressing floors; notice how water was brought down from the leats (by pipe) to power this operation. A Pelton wheel is a type of dynamo that runs at high speed and requires a good head of water.

THE COT VALLEY

By comparison with the coast, the valleys which run down to it are little-known to walkers; many of them, in fact, are almost impenetrable, or if they lead to a good beach are spoilt for walking by busy roads. As already mentioned with reference to Nanquidno, they can be places of great beauty, however, with micro-climates which encourage plant and animal life in total contrast to the cliffs close by; and for those interested in mining history almost every one of them along the north coast of Penwith is fascinating.

The Cot stream was undoubtedly a source of alluvial tin over many centuries; it requires a practised eye to find evidence on the ground, but some small dumps of a shape known as "whaleback", containing water-rounded stones, have survived near the mouth of the stream, and what Adam Sharpe describes as "the massive scarps on the valley sides" show "how much of the valley bottom has been scoured away." The streamers would have used the flowing water to wash the tin-bearing gravel they recovered after any necessary stamping in machines driven by waterwheels, but all remains of these operations have been obliterated by the elements and later industry. The Cot Valley is exceptionally rich in remains of stamping mills and dressing floors; most of them date from the middle of the 19th century but some are clearly more recent than that.

The Archaeological Unit's survey is particularly interesting in its study of the leats on the southern slopes, "which give an exceptionally dramatic impression of the long importance of water power in this mining district." Four main leats are identified, the lowest of which are entirely within the valley and may be associated in part with early tin streaming, but the highest two not only supplied the tinworks in the valley but also ran round the headland to serve waterwheels on and below the cliffs. The top leat begins well to the north of the Cot Valley, bringing in water from a smaller stream near Bosorne Farm. In a few places the water from the adits of mines on the south side, such as Letcha, the Reens and South Wheal Rose, was probably fed into the system. Maximum use seems to have been made of every drop of water, with many ponds holding reserves, and the tailrace from one waterwheel being led to another at a lower level wherever possible.

8 **Climb the steps beside the stamps foundations and turn left on the path above, then keep to the higher path.** The concrete dressing floors on the other side of the valley, including a convex buddle, are relics of fairly recent mining. You will also see adit portals and shallow excavations beside the road, as well as heaps of mine waste, and several ruined buildings half-buried in vegetation nearer the stream, remains of earlier mining operations. On this side ran the long leats that served the many waterwheels in the valley and on and below the cliffs; in places the courses of these leats have been obscured by later mining, or they have been adapted as paths or tracks. The substantial ruined walls down by the stream once enclosed dressing floors; a big wheelpit has survived. **Continue along the upper path until you have passed Cot Valley Lodge and some cottages, then descend to the valley bottom.**

9 Don't cross the stream, but take the signed path on the right just before the bridge.

Before doing so, however, have a good look at the ruined granite building on your right. It was not a cottage, but housed a set of water-driven stamps. The wheelpit is still clear to see (on the side of the building nearest the path), and so are two small concave buddles and one much larger convex one. From the last a small tailings leat runs back to the stream. This group of structures is probably the best preserved - certainly the most accessible - of three stamping mills located in the Cot Valley by the Archaeological Unit. This one is shown on the 1st edition OS map of 1876 as still operating, but had evidently ceased by the time surveying was carried out for the 1906 edition.

The path starts with a few rough steps, then becomes very narrow as it runs beside a wall. It curves left and crosses the stream on a footbridge (look left for a good example of exotic garden plants flourishing in the valley microclimate mentioned earlier)**. Up a few more steps, then turn left at the wider path. Keep right at the next junction. At the top, turn left, and from there return to the car park in St Just by the same route as you began the walk.**

The King's Arms and St Just Parish Church

WALK 6
ST JUST, THE COT VALLEY, CAPE CORNWALL
& THE KENIDJACK VALLEY (SOUTH)
Nearly five miles

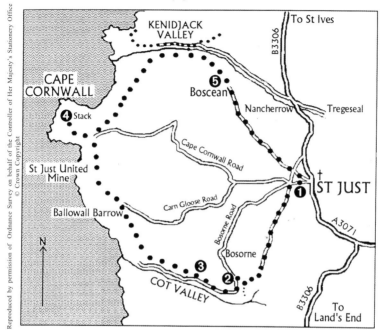

Scenically this is perhaps the most satisfying and varied of all the walks near St Just, because it starts and ends with contrasting valleys, between which come fine cliffs with superb views, and one of the county's deservedly most famous places, Cape Cornwall. It also includes the most impressive prehistoric monument in this district.

There are few if any steep climbs on this walk, and you are not likely to encounter problems with mud or overgrown paths or stiles. Pubs and toilets are available only in the town.

Readers wanting more detailed information about St Just United and Cape Cornwall mines are referred to *Exploring Cornish Mines* Volume 5.

Directions start from the main car park in St Just: details as for Walk 5.

1 Follow the directions in the first section of Walk 5, but this time ignore the stile ahead, overlooking the Cot Valley mills: turn right, taking the rough, downhill path. When you reach a granite standing stone in the middle of the path, continue for about another ten yards,

then turn right. **This path soon slopes down to meet a minor road.
2 Turn left on that. After a few yards it curves right and heads down
the Cot Valley towards the sea.** (See the note about the Cot Valley on
pages 58-59.) **Continue along the road for a quarter of a mile or so.
3 Take the signed coastal footpath - a widish track going up on the
right** which soon passes a surprisingly fertile-looking vegetable garden,
islanded amidst the bracken. Higher up are waste heaps and many shafts,
some unusually close together and all surrounded now by barbed-wire
fences plus impressive walls. Looming ahead is the tall, rather insecure-
looking chimney which was once part of the whim-engine house of
Bosorne and Ballowall Mine.

BOSORNE AND BALLOWALL MINE

*"The describing of an area of mining remains as complex, multi-phased
and overgrown as Ballowall has proved a truly daunting task," writes
Adam Sharpe - and, believe me, he is not easily daunted! The area along
the north side of the Cot Valley and as far along the coast as Carn Gloose
was probably mined from prehistoric times till as recently as the 1940s. A
bewilderingly large number of small mines were at work at different times,
most of which were known by various names (seven variations on
"Ballowall" are listed, for example), and they worked in several different
combinations. During some periods in the latter part of the 19th century
they were a part of St Just United or St Just Amalgamated - see the later
note. Although so few recognisable mine buildings have survived, there
is ample evidence among the furze and bracken and along the cliffs and
valley-sides to show how intensively the area was worked: Mr Sharpe
mentions 17 adits and 106 shafts - but how many others have escaped
attention so far? "The ground on this common," wrote R.M.Ballantyne in
"Deep Down" (1868), " is so riddled with holes of all sizes and shapes,
utterly unguarded by any kind of fence, that it requires care on the part of
the pedestrian who traverses that place even in daylight." There are plenty
of fences now, and walls, but the warning is still very relevant.*

**The coast path runs well to the left of this stack; I suggest that instead
you go a little further inland to join the minor road that runs beside it.
Take the first path heading inland after seeing the stack, and turn left
at the junction with another path, joining the road where there is a**

public seat. The road takes you beside the stack, with the scanty remains of its engine house, and then to one of the most impressive prehistoric monuments I know of, the magnificent Bronze Age chambered cairn known as the Ballowall Barrow.

BALLOWALL BARROW

The name is said as "Bal-owl". Perhaps the word is linked with "bal", a mine: John Norden (c.1584) mentions "Ball-luholl" in St Just as one of the main mines of Penwith. The barrow is sometimes referred to as Bollowall, Carn Gluze or Carn Gloose. It is a huge and, so far as is known, unique chamber tomb of very early date - Neolithic and Bronze Age, probably about 2,500 - 1,500 BC. The central chamber, which originally seems to have had a dome-like roof, contained several stone coffins; it is surrounded by a massive wall, 8 feet high in places and 20 feet thick, apparently of later date, which has an entrance grave set into it. Ballowall Barrow, long buried twenty feet under mine dumps, was excavated in the 1870s. The excavators, described by Aileen Fox as a gang of miners, did a lot of reconstructing, and built a new wall around the central chamber so that it could be viewed more easily. In charge of the dig was W.Copeland Borlase, who wrote a blow-by-blow account of it which was published in the Journal of the Royal Institution of Cornwall in 1878-81; Ian Cooke gives a lively version of it in "Journey to the Stones", along with some speculation about the ceremonial significance of the cairn.

Continue to the end of the road, rejoining the coast path as it approaches Priest's Cove and Cape Cornwall. The few buildings that border the road as it runs down to Priest's Cove and the walled shaft nearer the sea belonged to the Little Bounds part of St Just United mine.

ST JUST UNITED MINE

This name was first applied to the many small - and in some cases probably very ancient - mines immediately south of Cape Cornwall in 1861. The photos in "Exploring Cornish Mines" Volume 5 showing a mass of mine buildings and machinery overlooking Priest's Cove are some of the most surprising old pictures of the St Just area, I think, because it requires a sharp eye now to detect any evidence of all that industry on the clifftop.

Payday at St Just Amalgamated (alias St Just United), photographed by Moody of Penzance in 1873. In the distance is Cape Cornwall Mine.

The mine had a chequered history in the 19th century, with quite short bursts of large-scale activity. There were some failed attempts to re-work the mine or its dumps in the 20th century, but the last significant phase in its history was the 1880s, when its underground levels were combined with those of Cape Cornwall Mine, extending inland to St Just town and under the sea to the Brisons. The likelihood of making big profits with a venture like this can be gauged by the fact that the company had to fence off and make safe literally hundreds of old shafts and surface workings, and pump nearly forty million gallons of water out of the deeper shafts and levels that had been abandoned in 1875. Even the discovery of a huge "shoot" of tin ore, as much as 60 feet wide and 150 feet high, and so rich that it was nicknamed the "Cream Pot", failed to save the mine from the effects of falling prices, and it closed in 1889.

Just before that, a novel called "Tin" was published under the pen-name Edward Bosanketh, which focused mainly on a mine called Redborne Consols, in reality St Just United, and caused such consternation by its highly plausible portrayal of corruption in high places that every available *copy was bought and burnt by the powerful Bolitho family. (See the Gulval walk in "A View from Trencrom".) For anyone who values the opportunity to understand the St Just mining landscape in terms of the men and women who created it, "Tin" is essential reading - luckily, it is also very entertaining.*

The tiny, ramshackle winch-house and fishermen's huts above the slip at Priest's Cove are worth a closer look. The huts are known locally as "crows" - the word rhymes with "cows" and means "hovels". Notice, too, the small bathing pool that has been created among the rocks, and the evidence of early mining in the west-facing cliffs above the beach. "The coastal stope on Saveall's Lode in Priest's Cove is one of the most dramatic and accessible of this type of feature anywhere in Cornwall," according to Adam Sharpe. The gate at its entrance, fitted by the National Trust, does not prevent you from seeing how large these workings are. The name of the cove is unlikely to refer to a clergyman, despite the closeness of a chapel in early times. Des Hannigan suggests it may derive from a Cornish word for meadow, but it is probably a corruption of "Porth Just", "P'r East". (Compare the old name of Gorran Haven, Port East, which refers to the tiny church there, dedicated to St Just.)

Continue up the impressive flight of steps. The way up to the mine stack perched with perfect aesthetic judgement on the summit of the Cape is obvious, and a National Trust sign offers you the choice of steep and gentle ascents. Unsurprisingly, the stack was part of Cape Cornwall Mine. When looking north-west from there you can clearly make out the remains of leats on the cliffs on the southern side of the next (Kenidjack) valley. Cape Cornwall's old name was Kilguth East ("East" again referring to St Just); the honour of being called a Cape is said to derive from the fact that it was once believed to be the most westerly point on the English mainland, marking the boundary between the English Channel and St George's Channel.

CAPE CORNWALL MINE

Though much restored in later years, the famous chimney on the summit has been there for nearly a century and a half. Originally it was linked by a long flue to a winding-engine house on the south side, but the draught it created was too fierce for the boiler, and a smaller stack just above the engine house was built to replace it. It had proved a useful navigational aid, however, and was kept. Jack Trounson in 1982 described it as "in a bad state of repair", but it was restored in 1986 by the National Trust.

Mining probably took place on the Cape quite early, but Cape Cornwall Mine dates from 1836; it then worked, intermittently and sometimes under different names, till 1875. Its last active period was as part of St Just United (1879-89). Old photographs taken from Priest's Cove or the cliffs to the south reveal a scene scarcely less spectacular than the Crowns at Botallack, with the headgear of the pumping-engine house on the very edge of the cliff at the tip of the Cape. The one reproduced here, dating from 1880, also shows the long, curving flue linking the whim engine to the stack on the top; on the right is the small gunpowder magazine.

Apart from the stack, and the imposing count house beside the path leading up to it, little now remains of the mine's buildings. The long walls enclosing terraces below the count house look remarkably similar to some mine buildings elsewhere - the Vanner House at Wheal Basset, Carnkie, for example - but in fact they were built as part of a vinery. This is, though, where the mine's dressing floors were. Another relic that has survived is the base of a small circular gunpowder magazine like the two at Botallack; it is close to the easier path to the top but obscured by vegetation. The cylinder bolts of the 40-inch pumping engine out on the headland are still visible in the path that leads round to the coastguards' lookout.

4 To continue the walk, you have to return along the road on the southern side of the Cape.

In a field on your left is a small farm building on the site of the medieval

St Helen's Chapel, sometimes called St Catherine's Oratory. The small cross on it is not as old as it looks. When you reach the toilet block, it's worth going through the gate opposite and taking the path to the little building, especially for the fine view you get from it of the seaward end of the Kenidjack Valley, where the wheelpits and other relics of Boswedden Mine stand. (The stile at the field corner beyond gives access to paths along the north side of the Cape and down to the boulder-strewn beach of Porthledden Cove.)

Ahead as you continue along the road is Porthledden House, built by Francis Oats (1848-1918), a Botallack miner who, having achieved impressive exam results in Mineralogy, went out to the South African diamond mines, grew rich, returned home and bought Cape Cornwall in the early 1900s.

The coast path continues below the house's grounds, in which there appear to be old mine burrows or the remains of quarrying, **and past a lonely house named Wheal Call**, with its magnificent view across Porthledden Cove. ("Porthledden" probably means "wide cove". For Wheal Call, see the note on Boswedden Mine, page 76.) **Soon the coast path curves inland at the seaward end of the Kenidjack or Nancherrow Valley,** giving you a bird's-eye view of some of the surface remains of Boswedden Mine. As you walk further inland, notice the pattern of small square or triangular fields on the opposite slopes - probably a survival from very early times. Ahead in the valley-bottom are the ruined buildings of the arsenic works, its tall stack wearing an odd little crooked cap.

THE KENIDJACK ARSENIC WORKS

It is of special interest because the remains include those of a Brunton calciner and "lambreth" flues much older than the famous ones at Botallack. Arsenic works always had tall stacks in order to create the necessary draught, but the extra-tall one here was built, I presume, in the hope of reducing the effects of noxious fumes in the valley; and the unusual cowl, which looks as if it may soon drop off, is supposed to have been needed because of the risk of downdraughts in this particular setting, or to direct the fumes away from crops on the nearby hillside.

Where the path divides, with the coast path starting its descent to the valley bottom, carry straight on, continuing at the high level. Soon this brings you right above the arsenic works stack.

The Kenidjack arsenic works. Early in 2004 work was getting under way to clear the invading scrub and stabilise the buildings.

On the other side of the valley are the buildings of Kenidjack Farm and hamlet, including the winding/pumping engine house of Wheal Drea (again visited on the next walk); much less complete but still a prominent landmark on the skyline further left is the stamps engine house of Wheal Grouse, which like Wheal Drea became part of Wheal Owles; and close at hand is the small stack of (Lower) Boscean Mine. (Hereabouts when my late wife Viv and I did this walk we chatted with a man - about 60 years of age, I'd guess - who told us that he was born less than three miles away and had worked as a miner at Geevor till it closed. Now that he had some time to spare he was exploring the area and was bowled over by all the things he was seeing. Only yesterday he had visited the Cot Valley for the first time! On the other hand, he was quite familiar with Bavaria ...)

BOSCEAN MINE

An important lode of copper and tin, very unusual in that much of it runs north/south instead of north-west/south-east, was mined under the sea by the Crowns section of Botallack, and it also lies beneath the Boscean district. This is one of the oldest mining setts in the area, mentioned in 1584 by John Norden, and during the 19th century it was worked on a large scale, employing at least seven beam engines. The chimney of one engine house and the ruins of the arsenic works are still important landmarks; beside the Kenidjack stream are remains of water-driven stamps and dressing floors; but surprisingly little else can now be seen on the surface. More than meets the eye has probably survived, however, buried beneath dense scrub and the farm rubbish near Boscean hamlet.

Two incidents of special interest took place in 1857 and about ten years later. On both occasions, miners at Boscean accidentally broke into other workings. Two men drowned that first time; the second accident killed no-one but resulted in heavy losses for Boscean, because Wheal Owles alleged "theft" of 15 fathoms of mineral ground, and Boscean was not only fined £600 but forced to hand over a section of its own workings, Lower Boscean, complete with all fixtures and fittings. The injustice of this became all-too-apparent over 25 years later, long after Boscean had closed, when one of the worst disasters in Cornish mining history afflicted Wheal Owles because of its own purser's failure to make accurate plans of the mine's workings. See the note on Wheal Owles, pages 79-80.

5 **As you approach the stack, keep to the upper track, which curves right and passes among the houses of Boscean** (Cornish, "dwelling in the dry place", pronounced "B'see -un"). The 17th-century Boscean farmhouse has been converted and extended to accommodate Scott Marshall's pottery. **Now the track becomes a minor road.** Notice the former count house (offices) of Boscean Mine, on the right. Soon after you enter St Just you will pass the rear of Cape Cornwall School (comprehensive), and nearby on your left is the large Wesleyan Methodist Church, built in 1833 and enlarged in 1860 to accommodate anything up to a thousand people. ("Emigrants say that the big chapel at St Just is the last piece of the Old Country they see as the liners from Southampton and Plymouth turn on their straight course for America, and the first they see on their return" - so wrote the Superintendent of the St Just Circuit on the occasion of the chapel's centenary.) **Continue ahead at the crossroads, and you will come to Bank Square. On the right, beside the war memorial clock tower, is the Plen an Gwary. Take the path through that, and turn right at the street to return to the car park.**

PLEN AN GWARY

This is a fascinating place with a very long and varied history. Ian Cooke argues that its origins may be prehistoric, since its shape and size are typical of many ancient ceremonial circles, and its Bank Square entrance faces the midsummer sunrise. Certainly it is at least medieval, and as an

The Plen an Gwary, with Bank Square behind. The holes in the granite blocks are a relic of hand-drilling contests.

arena for the performance of plays - five manuscripts of Cornish "miracle plays" (Ordinalia) have survived - it was once just one of many in Cornwall. All but one of the others exist now only on paper and in place-names like Plain an Gwarry in Redruth and Playing Place on the Truro-Falmouth road; Piran Round near Perranporth is the only other one still intact and still occasionally used as a theatre. (See Walk 3 in "Around St Agnes & Perranporth".) The literal translation of "plen an gwary" is "arena of the play" in the sense of drama, but the St Just arena is probably typical in having been the setting for "play" in the sense of contests of many sorts: wrestling, athletics, tests of strength and bravery - even duels, though they hardly come under the heading of "play". When William Borlase saw it in the 18th century it was still in good order, with six tiers of stone seating all round the central performing space, and was the obvious choice of venue for religious meetings: both the Wesley brothers preached here. A century later, though still occasionally used by visiting preachers and by miners for rock-drilling contests, it had degenerated into a town tip, and almost all trace of the seating had gone. Our own age has restored something of its old importance and function: parts of an English version of the Ordinalia have been performed there again each summer since 2000, the Cornish Gorsedd ("meeting of bards") has assembled there - and it has even found a new role as a helicopter pad!

WALK 7
ST JUST, THE KENIDJACK VALLEY (NORTH), BOTALLACK AND LEVANT

About 7 miles; or it could be shortened in various ways, for example reducing it to about 3½ miles by starting at Botallack Mine and omitting both Levant and St Just. Directions are also given for a round walk taking in only Botallack and Levant.

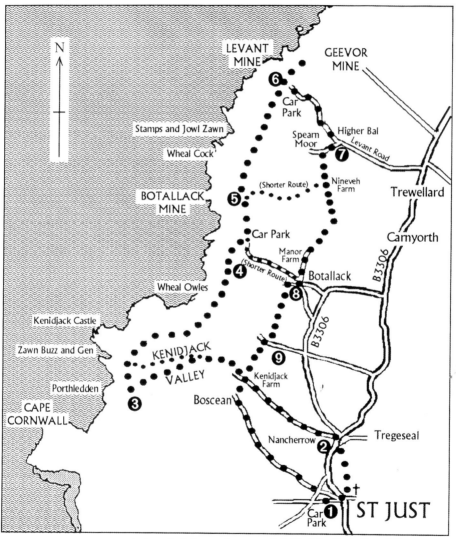

A walk that includes the Kenidjack (Nancherrow) Valley, Botallack and Levant Mines will scarcely need recommending to anyone with the slightest knowledge of Cornish scenery or Cornish mining. I'm sure you could walk this route a hundred times without noticing everything of historical interest. If possible, choose a day when the whim engine at Levant is in steam: Fridays from March to October are a fairly safe bet, but for full details ring 01736-786156 or 01736-796993. For more information about the mines in this area, see *Exploring Cornish Mines* Volumes 1 and 3. A guided tour of Geevor Mine is also included in the latter book; I have omitted it here because it really needs a full-day visit to do justice to the museum and the underground and surface tours.

This is a longer and tougher walk than the others in this book: ideally, allow a full day for the complete route, especially if a visit to the restored steam engine at Levant is to be included. There are some steep climbs along the coast and probably plenty of mud on the field paths inland. To enjoy the best of the cliff scenery you need a good head for heights; dogs and young children must be kept under strict control for their own safety.

There are no pubs, cafés, shops or public toilets on the route except in St Just, but the Queen's Arms in Botallack village is close to the inland section and only a few hundred yards from the clifftop part of Botallack Mine. Refreshments and toilets are also available at Geevor Mine.

Park in St Just, as directed for the previous two walks. Alternatively, park at Botallack Mine, which would increase your options for shortening the walk. For this, take either of the roads towards the coast from Botallack village, on the B3306 about a mile north of St Just. The roads meet and become a rough track leading to quite a large parking area on the right just past the Botallack count house, i.e. before you reach the prominent headgear at Allen's Shaft. (Trackside parking further on, which many drivers prefer if they want to admire the view without leaving their cars, is causing severe erosion, and therefore will be avoided by the kind of person I am writing this book for.) For this version of the walk, pick up the directions part-way through the first paragraph in point 4, where the parking space is mentioned.

There is another convenient car park at Levant Mine, which is at the coastal end of a minor road leaving the B3306 at Trewellard, beside a large chapel. The turning is about a quarter of a mile after the main entrance to Geevor Mine if you are approaching from the St Ives direction. The directions start at point 6 if you choose this option.

WALK 7

1 Starting at St Just, turn right on leaving the car park (Market Street), and at Market Square continue ahead past the King's Arms towards the church.

ST JUST CHURCH - AND ST JUST THE MAN

This grey, sturdy building may not be very different from many another old church in Cornwall, but it has a particularly strong appeal for me - largely, I suspect, because it seems so well suited to its setting within the hilltop town among the other bleak, windswept hills of its parish. The forthright plainness of its outside appearance is offset by the ornate south porch that was added early in the 16th century, some 150 years after the bulk of the building was done. Inside, the church is a little disappointing, since it was thoroughly restored in 1865 according to the tastes of J.P. St Aubyn, who scraped off nearly all the plaster and replaced floor, roof, pews and glass. Luckily, a little old plaster was retained on the north wall, where parts of six medieval paintings had been hidden under whitewash ever since Henry VIII's decree of 1547 had required that all such "popery" be obliterated. The Victorian restorers considered two of them, "St George and the Dragon" and "Christ of the Trades", worthy of preservation. An interesting leaflet about the wall paintings is (I hope) on sale in the church, together with a very full guide to the church as a whole. The latter draws attention to the beautiful 15th-century carvings on the sandstone piers, and tells of the discovery within the building in 1834 of the "Silus Stone", a headstone bearing the "Chi-Rho" Christian monogram and a Latin inscription. It is thought to date from the 5th century, and Charles Henderson in his "Cornish Church Guide" suggested that the inscription, "Selus ic iacit" ("Selus lies here"), "may prove to commemorate Selef, brother of St Just". St Just or Iestyn and his brother were said to be sons or grandsons of the "king" or chieftain Gerent, otherwise known as St Geraint and as Sir Geraint in the Arthurian legends. His home was supposed to have been near Gerrans in the Roseland, so it is no surprise that the other two Cornish churches dedicted to St Just are nearby, at St Just in Roseland and Gorran Haven. Just and his brother, however, apparently wandered further west: Selef, otherwise known as Seleven, lent his name to the parish of St Levan (see Walk 3), and it was claimed in early times that Just was buried at "Lafrouda", now known as St Just in Penwith. As with so many Cornish saints, lack of knowledge about their lives has opened the door to plentiful speculation.

Take the footpath on the left beside the gate into the churchyard.
Several of the headstones here reflect the grim reality of life and death in
a mining community; one, for example, which lies prone and is partially
covered with turf, reads, *"To the Memory of Edward Victor, who was
accidentally killed in the Boscaswell Mine May the 31st 1832 aged 48
years. Also of John his son who was accidentally killed in the Botallack
Mine June the 14th 1852 aged 22 years".*

**Once you have passed the pretty granite cottages of Church Square
the path is very obvious, running straight ahead and bringing you via
six Cornish stiles (granite cattle-grids) down to the main road (B3306)
at Tregeseal hamlet, opposite the attractive buildings of Nancherrow
Farm. Cross the road with care, and go a few yards to the right, over
the bridge.** On the opposite corner is the old toll house, now the Tregeseal
Gallery - a good place to buy original paintings and cards of the St Just
area, as well as other local products.

**2 Take the left turning, a narrow road leading down the Kenidjack or
Nancherrow Valley.** At the top is an impressive old barn, and a bob wall
overlooks the road. This is what remains of the stamps-engine house of
Wheal Grouse, part of Wheal Owles, built by 1857 - possibly as early as
1830 - for a 30-inch engine. (There is a note about Wheal Owles later.) A

*An undated photo of a tin-streaming operation, one of several formerly
in the Kenidjack Valley. The waterwheels were probably driving small
batteries of stamps. In the distance is the tall arsenic-works stack.*

pumping-engine house once stood beside it, but only the base of that remains. Beyond the small sewage works, the valley begins to be dominated by a mine dump up on the right. Soon you will reach the short row of terraced cottages, former almshouses, below the Wheal Drea engine house and the farm buildings of Kenidjack; up on the left is the small stack of Lower Boscean Mine. (See the note on pages 68-9.)

Don't cross the stream: continue down the valley road, now little more than a track, keeping left where there is a fork (NT Kenidjack sign). Next come the picturesque and historically important ruins of the Kenidjack arsenic works (pages 67-8). It appears to have treated arsenic from several local mines not big enough to have their own calciners. (See page 81 for some information about arsenic production.) **Still keep left, continuing beside the stream, and passing coast path signs left and right.** On the far side of the stream roughly opposite the right-hand coast path sign is the reservoir known as Catcher's Pool, originally the header pond for the Wheal Call waterwheel, whose big wheelpit will soon come into view. The lower end of this valley (pictured below) is one of my very favourite places, both for its beauty (especially in winter when the curse of Japanese knotweed is less obtrusive, the stream is in full spate, and the low sun casts dramatic shadows on Cape Cornwall and the craggy rocks closer at hand) and for the relics of Boswedden Mine which lie all around.

WALK 7
BOSWEDDEN MINE

It is safe to assume that miners have exploited this area for many centuries, but records go back only to 1782. The value of the Kenidjack / Tregeseal / Nancherrow / Boswedden stream (take your pick as to its name) for operating mills, both corn and stamping, was already fully exploited by the time the Rev. John Buller wrote about St Just (1840): "From this moor (Bostraze) flows a clear crystal stream of water, which maintains its purity, till it reaches the first mill in its winding course towards the sea. As it proceeds, it suspends a portion of the ochreous substance of the minerals, which are pounded and washed in numerous stamping mills to which it gives motion; till, by the time it reaches its destination, it becomes so turbid as to stain the sea ..." Adam Sharpe estimates that the stream may have driven 50 waterwheels including those at the St Just Foundry. What was probably the largest waterwheel ever erected in Cornwall - 65 feet in diameter - was in use at Wheal Call (later part of Boswedden Mine) by 1837. The magnificent wheelpit that stands near the mouth of the valley now is not big enough to have contained it: that seems to have been built for a 30ft. wheel and to have been enlarged to accommodate a 52ft. wheel some time before 1865, which drove nearby buddles as well as operating pumps in two shafts by means of flat-rods. By this time the mine was exploiting mineral lodes under the sea, had a work force of 155, and employed five steam engines, two of which operated only when conditions were too dry for the waterwheels.

Rather surprisingly, perhaps, Boswedden was never very profitable, and its workings were closed down in the mid-1870s. The flash flood that resulted from the thaw after the Great Freeze of 1892 destroyed many of the smaller mining structures that still remained in the valley; some of the larger ones were used for demolition practice during World War 2; and the rest would probably have vanished in recent years if Geevor's plans to rework the dumps had been realised.

It's well worth crossing the stream if you can find a safe place to do so, because the huge wheelpit over there, built with dressed granite, is among the most impressive and best preserved in Cornwall. By the use of flat-rods, one of which passed through the small tunnel you will notice beside the stream, the 52-foot-diameter wheel there during the 1860s drove the pumps in two mineshafts, one upstream and the other nearer the sea. On the slope behind it (and just visible in the top-left-hand corner of the

photo) is the ruined pit of a 30ft. wheel which drove "Water Whim", used for hauling skips in the Wheal Call diagonal shaft, now marked by a very large waste tip. The water that drove this wheel then passed over the larger one below. The ruined engine house among the dressing floors on the same (south) side contained a 28-inch beam engine for working the stamps and also for winding. Since so much water power was usually available here, steam engines did not often have to be used; even so, there was also a 37 or 40-inch one available for pumping, and the foundations of the house built for that are close to the track, on the right among the big spoil heaps. Both these engine houses were used by US Army engineers for demolition practice shortly before D-Day.

As you reach the rocks above the beach (Porthledden), notice the remains of buddles; half of one of them has disappeared over the low cliff. Down by the beach a small building, now partly demolished, originally housed a water turbine known as a Pelton wheel, probably installed by a hotel above to supply electricity. Catcher's Pool was reinstated to serve as the header pond for it, long after the Wheal Call waterwheel fell out of use. The diesel engine whose remains are in the building was installed to replace the Pelton wheel, or to supplement it in dry periods.

3 Next comes a stiff climb to the clifftop. You could go back up the valley-track and take the signed coast path, but the best way, if you don't mind a very steep climb and a scramble or two, is the first little path you come to (just beyond the engine house on the opposite side). This takes you across the dumps, where there are many interesting specimens of mineralised rock brought up by the miners, and at a higher level you pass beside a fenced gunnis. Further up again, a small side path gives you the chance to peer out above Zawn Buzz and Gen, if you have the nerve for it. (Zawn is from the Cornish word for a cleft or chasm; the rest of the name is a puzzle, but Weatherhill suggests "giant's dwelling".) During one of the breathers you will probably need to take as you continue upwards, look back to the opposite side of the valley: from here you can clearly see the various leats, similar to those on the same side of the Cot Valley. Most of them supplied the many waterwheels in the valley, but the highest continued right round to Cape Cornwall Mine to drive the stamps there.

When you reach a wide track you need to go a few feet to the right and continue uphill on the signed coast path; but first you might be interested to look at the Kenidjack Quarries, around to the left. They were once linked to the B3306 by a tramway, parts of which can still be traced. These greenstone quarries were much in the news during the 1980s and early '90s owing to the eviction from them of a group of travellers who had set up their distinctive little "bender" homes there. **At the clifftop a stile enables you to cross a stone wall; then head for the coast-path post to the right of the ruined building.** Adam Sharpe suggests this may have been the quarry manager's house and quarry offices, but Kenneth Brown thinks it more likely to be associated with the nearby rifle ranges.

Scattered all over this clifftop area are relics of many different periods and enterprises, some of them very hard to make sense of now. Beside the building is a small Early Bronze Age circle, at the centre of which was once a burial chamber; nearby are the ramparts of the Iron Age fortification known as Kenidjack Castle; a mine named after that, Wheal Castle, has left various fragments such as the base of an engine house and a small pond (now dry) which held water for its boiler; and the most substantial ruins are the remains of the St Just Battery, which operated from about 1870 to the early 1900s. The firing positions and especially the butts (revetted with masonry, some of it taken from the engine house) are still clear to see.

Although so little is left of the Wheal Castle engine house, something of its history is, I think, worth including here. It was built in 1883 for a rotative engine, about 22-in., "in connection with a short-lived reworking intended to open up an intersection between two important lodes under the sea a short way out from the cliff. The method used was remarkable. Instead of rehabilitating an old shaft ... above adit level, the skip road and pump rods were taken out and down the sheer face of the cliff! Then they entered the adit a short distance and were turned down the shaft which was enlarged to receive them. Fixing the installations, including a ladder road, down a windswept cliff with Atlantic breakers below is a feat which is better imagined than described!" (The quotation is from a set of notes provided by Kenneth Brown for one of his field-trips.)

As the path approaches Botallack Mine there is a choice of ways, both of which have much to offer as they pass through an area that is bewilderingly rich in remains of mining enterprises ancient and modern. To attempt to describe and explain everything would be to overload a book intended to be easily portable, and probably succeed only in confusing you, so I shall concentrate on the most prominent features.

The first two are engine houses dating from about 1870, relics not of Botallack but of Wheal Owles.

WHEAL OWLES & THE 1893 DISASTER

Like most if not all the other mines hereabouts, Wheal Owles consisted of a combination of many small old mines; for example, one called "Whele an Houl" ("Owles" derives from Cornish "als", meaning cliff or shore) was at work by 1725.

The period of Wheal Owles' greatest prosperity was the 1860s, when it had 11 engines and what Adam Sharpe describes as "the staggering total of 29 miles of levels, 3 miles of adits, and an additional mile of levels being driven each year". Poor prices for metallic ores during the '70s and '80s led to the closure of most of the inland sections of the mine; the best prospects seemed to be under the sea. In 1884 the decision was taken to focus all efforts on the Cargodna section, and the clifftop pumping engine there was the only one that continued working.

It was just before 9am on 10th January 1893 that miners broke through into the flooded 148 fathom level of Wheal Drea - which according to the plans they were relying on was nearly 40m away from where they were working. The torrent of water that surged through the new levels with a roar described by one of the survivors as "louder than ten thousand thunders" was so devastating that, it is said, it created enough air pressure to blow out a big crater near the Kenidjack almshouses. Nineteen men and a boy were drowned - their bodies have never been recovered - and the management soon gave up any attempt to drain the mine. Cyril Noall gives a particularly vivid account of the bravery and practical intelligence of James "Farmer" Hall, who saved the lives of at least five men. He tells of the young miner called Thomas who was due to be married that day. The wedding was postponed at the Vicar's request, and Thomas was among those who died. One miner, Thomas Lutey, had had forebodings of tragedy, and for several days beforehand had taken to running through the workings shouting "Water! Water!" In the event, Thomas and his brother Richard narrowly escaped with their lives, but Thomas never went underground again. He earned a meagre living selling oranges in and around St Just, "walking along the roads with a shuffling gait, his eyes always fixed on the ground, as if he were expecting the earth to open under his feet."

On the left is the stamps engine house of Cargodna and Wheal Edward (which became part of Wheal Owles), stabilised by the National Trust in 1994. This engine house was sited to draw from Cargodna shaft partway down the cliff using an upright axle cage on the seaward side of the house. It was from that shaft that the twenty doomed miners made their final trip into the workings on that January morning. In 1993 a plaque

Wheal Edward stamps-engine house in 1991, before stabilisation. Botallack in the distance

commemorating the dead men was fixed to the wall surrounding it by members of the Carn Brea Mining Society. All around the engine house are many features of considerable historical interest, detailed in *Exploring Cornish Mines*, Volume 1. The tall fragment of wall roughly half-way between the two buildings is almost all that remains of a later whim-engine house; this also hauled from the Cargodna shaft, enabling the Wheal Edward engine to specialise in driving stamps.

The second building, also recently stabilised, is the Cargodna pumping engine house of Wheal Owles. A 36" beam engine was installed to pump from it. Attached to the main building are the remains of its boiler house.

4 A little further along are 19th-century dressing floors of Botallack Mine - you may be able to make out the remains of buddles: heath fires in the hot summer of 1995 revealed many such features formerly hidden.

The notes about Botallack and Levant mines are at the end of the directions for this walk (pages 92-8). Please bear in mind that at both sites work is, or is soon likely to be, in progress to stabilise buildings, excavate areas previously buried or overgrown, and so forth; one possible result is that the routes I suggest may in future need modification.

The tall stack marks one of the most impressive and in its way beautiful relics at Botallack, the arsenic works, built soon after the mine was re-opened in 1906: not even at Wheal Busy or Poldice are there such complete remains of a "lambreth".

Until the early 19th century, the arsenic content of ore was regarded as a menace because it spoilt the tin for smelting, so the stamped ore was roasted in "burning houses" and the noxious substances given off (sulphur as well as arsenic) were consigned to the atmosphere where they could supposedly do no harm. In order to collect the arsenic, basically all that was needed was to attach a very long flue to the calciner with a tall chimney at the end to provide a strong draught. As the gases cooled the arsenic condensed and formed crystals on the walls of the flue. When sufficient had collected, the calciner was stopped, iron doors in the flue were opened, and the arsenic "soot" was swept or shovelled out. To gain the maximum length of flue within a limited space, it was usually built in a zig-zag form, known as a labyrinth ("lambreth" in Cornwall). Botallack's was about 750 feet long. Finally the "soot" had to be treated at a refinery.

The building with a rather shapely arch a little below the flues housed a Brunton calciner, equipped with a slowly rotating hearth; beneath it is the power vault. Nearby are concrete dressing floors dating from the same period, with the massive foundations for Californian stamps above; all this was originally enclosed in a big mill building. Further up again, beside the pot-holed road leading inland, is the Botallack Count House, nicely restored. In the 1960s it was used as a folk-music venue; more recently as a restaurant; now it is a "multi-purpose community facility" and information centre run by the National Trust and a base for the Trust's local area warden. Alongside the parking space to the left of that some walls survive of the smith's shop, fitting shop, traction engine house, sawmill and men's dinner house - all built early last century, as was the tall chimney nearby. The modern headgear was erected in 1983 when the management at Geevor decided to re-open Allen's Shaft. The plan was to dewater it and clear away rubble down to 900 feet and then sink a new inclined shaft down to 2,000 feet to intersect with the Wheal Owles lodes under the sea. The 1985 crash in tin prices put paid to this scheme.

A track leads down, past Wheal Hazard Shaft, to the part of the mine that takes its name from the offshore islands, The Crowns, where still perch the most etched, drawn, painted and photographed engine houses in Cornwall: the Crowns pumping-engine house, built for a 36" engine about 1835 to replace another which had been there since at least 1816, and just above that the winding-engine house, built in 1862. The famous wooden skip-road shown in photographs taken at or around the time of the royal visit of 1865 (one is included in the later note about Botallack, page 93) ran from that across the cliff face down into the new Boscawen Diagonal Shaft, which had been sunk to 225 fathoms (1350 feet) below the adit near the bottom of the cliff. From the level area just below the winding-engine house you can see the mouth of Diagonal Shaft on the rock-face below. The bottom of the shaft is under the sea, over half a mile from the shore.

At this point you might find it helpful to refer to the 1850s engraving on the next page, showing the situation just before the Diagonal Shaft was sunk. The large headframe on the lower cliff-edge to the right was at Wheal Hazard Shaft; from that, overhead cables were carried up to a winding engine on the top which stood a little too far back from the edge to be visible in this view. The Crowns winding- / stamps-engine house is shown on the clifftop: some details about this are given later. Closest to

An 1850s engraving of Botallack mine

the sea is the Crowns pumping-engine house, and just visible around the corner, half-way up the cliff, is the winding-engine house on Wheal Button Shaft. The gabled building underneath the Crowns whim may have housed mine offices or provided miners' accommodation.

Return to the main track at the top and continue north. Notice the excavation on the inland side of the track, close to the coast path sign. Known as Grylls Bunny, it is a good example of "openwork", and may be a relic of some of the earliest mining in this area. The pit remains quite impressive despite the fact that material from Allen's Shaft was dumped in it during the 1980s, but the most interesting part of the Bunny is on the opposite side of the track, where several gunnises can be seen if you are prepared to scramble around on the rough little paths below. There is a "warren" of small chambers and tunnels, and this is thought by some to be the reason for the name, but the Cornish word "bonny", a bunch of ore, seems a more likely origin.

Not far past this, the coast path brings you to a small stack, all that remains - apart from a few foundations - of the Crowns whim-engine house, built in 1841. The main job of this engine in the early years was presumably to raise ore to the clifftop from the various shafts below, and a revetment wall on the edge of the cliff marks where the headframe for this purpose stood. After the sinking of the Diagonal Shaft it drew skips up and down a long, steep timber incline leading to a loading bay near the top of the Diagonal Shaft's own skip road. A gully in the cliff face -

not easily seen from the top - shows the course of the steeper skip road. The Crowns whim engine was also used to drive stamps, and at various periods it seems to have wound from Hazard Shaft and even from Wheal Cock, several hundred yards to the north.

One of the eye-bolts driven into the rock to help hold the steep wooden skip road in place

5 **Turn right beside the whim stack, following the coast path sign. Keep towards the right-hand side of the scrubby area. To reach the wide track you will probably have to clamber over some boulders, placed there presumably as a barrier against wheeled vehicles.**

If you do not want to visit Levant, go about four yards to the right, then take the path on the left (yellow arrow on wooden post). Now pick up the directions at 5a (page 90).

For the full walk to Levant, turn left along the wide track. You could now keep to the coast path; by doing so, however, you would miss the best scenery as well as some interesting and even breathtaking mining relics. In what follows, therefore, I suggest various side paths closer to the cliff edge, but please bear in mind that these may in places be unsafe in windy and/or wet conditions.

Almost immediately on your left you will notice a small stone bridge with an arched opening. The mines depended on a constant supply of clean water for their dressing floors and engines, and the miners skilfully and laboriously used to the full every drop available, creating reservoirs and building leats, sometimes several miles long. The leat which passed under the bridge, though dry now, can easily be followed as it runs north west towards the cliff edge through old dressing floors near the trig. point marker close to Botallack Head. This area was worked by Wheal Cock, which was already extracting copper and tin beneath the sea by 1778. It became part of Botallack after 1842. Much of the clifftop here is covered with mine waste - residue from the dressing of copper ore - and there is a large number of ruined buildings, foundations, masonry walls and so on, reflecting the complex history of this mine over two or more centuries.

If as you walk on you keep fairly near the cliff edge you will soon overlook one of the most awe-inspiring places I know, Wheal Cock Zawn and, just beyond it, Stamps and Jowl Zawn, easily recognisable by the natural arch on the far side of the wider inlet beyond. Its name is apt (Cornish, *stampes an dyowl sawn*, "The Devil Stamps Gully" - "stamps", of course, referring to Cornish stamps machines): beautiful though it is, the scenery might indeed be a fit home for the devil, and somehow its fearsomeness is redoubled by the evidence that men have delved into these rocks and under that sea. The mine's main shaft was close to the cliff edge at Wheal Cock Zawn, and a house for a 24" pumping engine stood beside it; Skip Shaft is higher up the cliff, and a 16" winding-engine house was provided for that. When Wheal Cock was reworked early in

the 20th century the stone from the pumping-engine house and other mine buildings such as the miners' dry, a smithy and stores, was used to build the massive retaining wall on the slope between the shafts plus linings inside the mouths of both shafts and walls around them. In the winter of 1992-3 these mouths were fitted with welded steel grills.

The Pathfinder map indicates a waterfall at Stamps and Jowl. This is not easily visible from above, but the two springs feeding the stream running to the cliff edge are easy enough to find as you walk on, and beside one of them is part of a low wall, the remains of a small dam. This water was needed at Levant mine, and the leat which carried it can be followed almost all the way. (If, however, you feel it looks too difficult or dangerous, use one of the paths at a higher level, which will take you beside or near a small round building, one of Levant's two explosives magazines.) Here and there the water in the leat had to be carried across small gullies by means of a launder hung on chains. Just above the natural arch and below Carn Vellan there is a small rock stack, and it appears that the miners blasted out a cleft behind that for the leat to pass through. The leat path gives a fine view of the far side of the arch, and later of several shafts. If you are taking this route, as you approach the mine buildings at Levant you need to veer a little to the right because the last few yards near the cliff edge above Boscregan Zawn are too dangerous to walk along. The water served the whim and pumping engines (the cooling pond beside the restored whim engine has been reinstated, and there are hopes that one day it will be supplied with water from its original source), but it seems that some of it was also carried further north-east, probably to a waterwheel at old dressing floors.

6 A visit to the refurbished whim engine house is not to be missed. Even if you cannot go inside to see the engine and boiler, it's worth walking around the sea-side of the building, past the pond just mentioned. Peer down over the retaining wall (can you work out how it was built?) and you will see the tortuous path down to the adit mouth not far above high-water level in Levant Zawn. Until it collapsed some fifty years ago, there was a spectacular bridge from the end of the path, along the west side of the zawn and into the adit. This was the normal method of entering the underground workings before the installation of the man engine - of which more later. Behind you, under the small headgear erected in recent years by Geevor, is the 278-fathom-deep Skip Shaft, in which skips were raised and lowered by the whim engine. (The answer to my quiz question a few lines back, by the way, is as follows: the cliff-edge was cut back to form a "plat" a few feet wide at the base of the intended wall, the building stone was lowered down to that, and the builders perched on the top of the wall as they built it. No need for safety nets, scaffolding or anything like that! The wall has recently been re-pointed by the volunteers restoring the Levant engine - all part of the service ...)

The tall ruined engine house is a very early one, built in 1835 for Levant's pumping engine, originally 40", later 45". The pumping shaft, now covered with a flat-roofed building, is very close to Skip Shaft but entirely separate. In recent years it was used to provide ventilation in the Geevor workings, and the building contains a fan for that purpose; the fan no longer operates, but steam often issues through the small gauze "roof", because the rock below is very hot. The rails a little further along are modern; the original tramway by which the ore raised in Skip Shaft was taken to the stamps ran in a tunnel under this area, and up the still visible incline. Workshops once stood on the concrete base beside the tramway.

Levant in the early 1920s
Left to right: Skip Shaft whim-engine house (where the preserved engine is);
calciner stack in distance; pumping-engine house with detached stack; stamps-engine house in distance; count house with smithy etc.; small round explosives magazine closer; power house / compressor house far right.

If possible continue along to the blackened arsenic stack near the cliff edge. (Early in 2004 the way there was barred because of excavation work in progress in and around the tunnel just mentioned, so we had to make a diversion up to the right.) The stack originally stood at the end of a long flue from the calciners whose remains can be seen in the distance.

The remains at Levant of one of the calciners (left) and a buddle (Photographs by Simon Jones)

After passing some ruined buddles, you are approaching the area now associated with Geevor Mine, where there is a complex mixture of old and new mining relics, including batteries of rectangular settling tanks and huge mounds of waste material.

I suggest you now turn back along the fairly wide track a little further inland, towards the car park which stands above the restored whim engine (point 6 on the map). Before reaching it you pass close to the stack which one served the stamps-engine house, the large power-house / compressor house with its tall chimney, and finally the group of buildings which include the former count house, the smithy and the miners' dry. This last, which stands beside the approach road, was where the miners changed their clothing and cleaned up after work: two sunken baths can be seen, near the spiral staircase by which the miners made their way to and from the top of Man-Engine Shaft. The staircase has recently been restored, and the tunnel leading to the shaft was being cleared when I was last at Levant.

Man-Engine Shaft itself - or at least the top of it - has been cleared and refurbished. It is visible from the car park, on the landward side, to the left of the short chimney-stack. Beside the stack are the concrete beds for the horizontal tandem compound engine which drove the man-engine; installed in 1893, it replaced a beam engine dating back to 1857. A photograph on page 177 of *Exploring Cornish Mines* Volume 3 shows the mouth of Man-Engine Shaft at the time of the 1919 disaster: see pages 97-8 in the later note about Levant.

For the inland walk to Botallack, the Kenidjack Valley and St Just, take the approach road from Trewellard, known as Levant Road.

Soon you reach what looks like a younger brother of the ramparts of the Plymouth barbican.

Photograph by Simon Jones

This massive wall, built to retain a huge pile of waste, includes two chutes which enabled ore to be loaded on to wagons, and a flight of steps leads up to one of the best-preserved of all the engine houses in the St Just area. It was built in 1887 for a 35" engine used for pumping and winding in the Guide Shaft of Levant Mine (Higher Bal). Part of the boiler house has survived, and it is easy to see where its lean-to roof was attached to the main building. Because of the two jobs the engine had to do, the structures (loadings) between the engine house and its concrete-capped shaft are unusually complex.

Continue for a few more yards towards Trewellard.

7 Take the first right turning, a wide track or dirt road leading to Nineveh Farm. Where there is a division of the ways, keep left - but you might choose to make a short diversion to the right first and cross the stile to see the scanty but still rather impressive remains of a stamps-engine house that belonged to Spearn Moor Mine, part of Spearn Consols, surrounded by the ruins of dressing-floor buildings. The Spearn mines, not among the most successful, produced mainly tin, and were eventually amalgamated with Levant. This engine house was built by 1878 for a 30" engine. **Return the same way and continue towards the farm. On reaching a farm gate, take the narrow path on the left side. Now watch for the granite stile on the right, some 20 yards beyond a telegraph pole.** Before you cross it, notice ahead the exceptionally small whim-engine house of Spearn Moor Mine, built for a 20" engine. It is probably over 150 years old, and therefore one of the earliest surviving engine houses in the district. **Continue along the left side of the field, and after two more stiles you are among the buildings of Nineveh Farm. Walk on straight ahead, cross the tumbledown stile between ruined buildings and walk with the hedge on your right. Now skip the next paragraph plus one sentence and pick up the directions at "Cross the next stile (with difficulty ..."**

5a *(The shorter walk route from Botallack, omitting Levant)* **Walk towards a farm gate, and take the path on the left just before that, where there is a metal bar to climb over or (more likely) duck under. After a few yards between hedges, follow the hedge on your right, heading just right of a mine stack. Where the hedge bends right, carry straight on to the field corner where there is a stile (beware of slippery stones). At the next field corner you have a rather steep, awkward stone stile, followed immediately by a wooden one. Now keep to the right-hand edge of the field, and continue towards the houses (Nineveh Farm), which you reach via a gate.** The stack was originally part of a whim engine house, built in 1882 on the Carnyorth section of Botallack Mine. (Just why a farm in Cornwall should appear to be named after an ancient Assyrian city I don't know. Could it be a corruption of the Cornish *ninnis*, meaning island or, if inland, a remote, isolated spot?)

Almost opposite the farmhouse, cross the tumbledown stile on the right between two ruined buildings and walk with the hedge on your right. Cross the next stile (with difficulty, I'm afraid, thanks to a wooden bar fixed above it) and then go very slightly left to a third one at the

corner; continue ahead with the hedge on your left to a fourth stile, a double one. Next the path goes slightly to the right. After a rather rough patch where brambles threaten to overgrow the path there is another stile. Now continue towards farm buildings, along the right edge of the next field, crossing one last stile (it's straight ahead, not really visible till you reach it) to join the muddy lane leading to Manor Farm. (Notice the well on the right immediately after crossing the stile.)

The exterior of the pretty house on the right at the end of the lane, with tall chimneys - the farmhouse of Manor Farm - was used as "Nampara" in the first series of "Poldark" on television. It dates from 1663.

If you started at Botallack or Levant and do not want to go on to the Kenidjack Valley and St Just, now turn right along the narrow road which passes by the farmhouse. The road soon diminishes to a wide track as it curves north, eventually taking you past Botallack count house to the car park. Turn to section 4 to continue with the descriptions and directions.

Otherwise, walk on ahead for a few more yards to the road junction. **8** At that point you could go straight on for the Queen's Arms; but to continue the walk turn right along a rough lane which soon runs beside newish bungalows, and take the narrow path on the left side of a granite house (Parknoweth Cottage was its name in 2004). After a stile the path crosses a small field to another stile. From there, continue in the same direction along a lane which runs up to a house beside a ruined engine house. This belonged to the original Wheal Owles and was built for a 36-inch pumping engine.

9 At the T-junction go a few feet right, towards the engine house, then left, along a signed footpath. After a stile the path runs between hedges; then cross another stile and go straight across the field ahead. After two more stiles the path brings you among the buildings of Kenidjack Farm, with the relatively well-preserved engine house on the left. It held a 26" engine used at different times to hoist and pump from two nearby shafts, both of which were on the Wheal Drea (pronounced "dray") section of Wheal Owles, the part that flooded after abandonment and brought about the 1893 tragedy. **Continue down to the valley road.**

If you started at Botallack or Levant and do not want to go on to St Just, now turn right, picking up the directions a little way into section 2.

For St Just, cross the bridge ahead and walk up the track with the Lower Boscean stack on your left. Go left at the top, through Boscean hamlet, completing the route back into the town as described at the end of Walk 6.

BOTALLACK MINE

In 1865 Thomas Spargo claimed that "The Botallack mine is probably the most remarkable in the world ... a wonder, showing the enterprise of man, and his marvellous control over the earth on which he moves."

There is little doubt that the Botallack area, where the mineral lodes were exceptionally prominent in the cliffs, was among the earliest to be mined in the St Just district. Nearly 30 small independent enterprises combined under the name of Botallack - many of them by the end of the 18th century, some others not until the start of the 20th. At least one of the small mines, Wheal Cock, had already driven levels under the sea by 1778, when in his "Mineralogia Cornubiensis" William Pryce wrote about the "thundering roar" of the Atlantic waves and the moving rocks on the sea bed heard by the miners below. "Add to this, that several parts of the Lode, which were richer than others, have been very indiscreetly hulked and worked within four feet of the sea; whereby, in violent stormy weather, the noise overhead has been so tremendous, that the workmen have many times deserted their labour under the greatest fear, lest the sea might break in upon them." For a colourful and humorous narrative showing how nerve-racking it was to be in that part of the mine even in calm weather, read Wilkie Collins' "Rambles Beyond Railways" (1851). Probably the earliest account we have of a visit to Botallack was published by Dr J.A.Paris in 1824, well before the existing pumping-engine house was built. "Surely," he wrote, "if ever a spot seemed to bid defiance to the successful efforts of the miner, it was the site of the Crowns Engine at Botallack, where at the very commencement of his subterranean labours, he was required to lower a steam engine down a precipice of more than two hundred feet, with the view of extending his operations under the bed of the Atlantic Ocean!!! ... In looking up you will observe troops of mules laden with sacks of coals, for the supply of the engine, with their undaunted riders, fearlessly trotting down the path which you trembled at descending even on foot. ... The workings of this mine extend at least seventy fathoms in length under the bed of the sea; and in these caverns of darkness are many human beings, for a small pittance, and even that of a precarious amount, constantly digging for ore, regardless of the horrors which surround them, and of the roar of the Atlantic ocean, whose boisterous waves are incessantly rolling over their heads."

   Cyril Noall's history of Botallack shows how the foresight and determination of one man, Steven Harvey James, kept it alive during hard times in the late 1830s, when prices were low and most of the tin and copper from the shallower levels had already been recovered, and ushered in the period of its greatest prosperity. Its first royal visitor was Queen Victoria, in 1846. From the late '40s onwards it expanded steadily, taking over several neighbouring mines and venturing much further under the sea with the aid of the Boscawen Diagonal Shaft, begun in 1858. Its name was a tribute to the owner of the mineral rights, Lord Falmouth. The descent of the new shaft by the Duke and Duchess of Cornwall (known elsewhere as the Prince and Princess of Wales) in 1865 went ahead despite a horrific accident in April 1863, when the chain attached to the iron gig broke as eight men and a boy were being hauled

The Crowns section of Botallack, thought to be at about the time of the royal visit in 1865. The pumping-engine house is on the right, with a capstan for hauling pitwork in Crowns Shaft. The newer whim-engine house stands at the top of the wooden skip-road serving Diagonal Shaft. The much steeper skip-road on the left was operated by another whim-engine on the cliff top.

to the surface. (Cyril Noall's "Cornish Mine Disasters" gives a long contemporary account in verse of "The Botallack Mine Tragedy", which includes the lines, "Young Peter Eddy's head was gone, Upon the skip he lay, The sollar struck him as they pass'd, And took his head away.") This event led to the substitution of wire rope for the chain: eventually chains were totally superseded by wire ropes throughout Cornwall and elsewhere.

Botallack became one of the most fashionable "attractions" in Cornwall; the opening of the through-line between Paddington and Penzance less than two years after the royal visit increased the flow of visitors. They were, as Noall puts it, "not altogether welcome," since they took up the valuable time of mine officials and occupied places in the gig that might more profitably have been taken by miners, so a fee of half a guinea was charged, the proceeds to be given to miners' widows and those maimed through working there.

After the '60s the mine's fortunes fluctuated, and problems caused by low prices or disappointing output were partly offset by sales of arsenic; but by the '90s so much cheap tin was being produced abroad that ruin was facing all Cornish mines, and when a cloudburst flooded the richest part of Botallack, Wheal Cock, in November 1894, followed by more underground flooding in February 1895, the mine's shareholders had no choice but to pay off the workforce and sell the surface plant.

Eleven years later came an ambitious attempt to re-open the mine, and most of the remains on the clifftop date from this period. Unfortunately, the lease granted to the new company by Lord Falmouth stipulated that a new shaft - known as Allen's, after Francis Allen, one of the directors - had to be sunk at the point where the modern headgear now stands. This was a bad mistake, because the best prospects for rich new discoveries of ore lay well out to sea. For three-quarters of a century from 1914 Botallack was abandoned to the elements. In 1980 - the year when Botallack received its third royal visitor, Queen Elizabeth II - Geevor Mine decided to extend its workings into Botallack, and efforts were made to refurbish Allen's Shaft, but the crash in tin prices of 1985 prevented any underground development from taking place. The latest news (February 2004) is that those concerned with a project called Waveshaft are considering using one of Botallack's shafts to generate electricity by harnessing the air currents of up to 100m per second created by waves crashing into and withdrawing from the caves below.

The best description of a visit to Botallack that I have read - and in fact *it beats all accounts I have read of visits to any mine - is that by J.R. Leifchild. No brief extract can do it justice: get a copy! It was Leifchild who told the story of the Blind Miner of Botallack, who knew the underground workings so intimately "that he became a guide to his fellow-labourers, if by any accident their lights were extinguished!"*

This engraving, published in "The Illustrated London News" in 1872, gives a good idea of the complexity of the mining operation at Botallack.

LEVANT MINE

"A shock, sudden and riveting, met my eyes on the next headland. From the edge of the cliff stretching inland and westward along the coast every spot of green has long been uprooted. Over all that headland was the ugly paraphernalia of an ancient mine in full working order. The sea at the base of the cliff is dyed red, the surface of the hill is rent and scarred, heaped high with rubbish, and from dingy chimneys black smoke issues. I heard the pounding of stamps, saw the conduits, the various receptacles where the tin is washed, and the ever-running discoloured water. This is the famous Levant Mine, whose working run for a mile or more under the sea." (C. Lewis Hind: "Days in Cornwall", 1907)

WALK 7

This was the greatest of all the St Just Mines (unless Geevor takes that honour by virtue of its production in the 20th century), and it has probably had more written about it than any other mine in Cornwall. Despite all that, its name remains a mystery. Its literal meaning, "rising" (hence the east, land of the rising sun), could perhaps have been chosen for its optimistic implications, like so many other Cornish mine names. Cyril Noall tentatively suggested that it might refer to the Levant Company, which traded - partly in tin - in the eastern Mediterranean towards the end of the Tudor period. If he is right, the antiquity of mining here seems to be indicated; but the earliest known reference to such mining dates from 1670, and the earliest recorded use of the name Levant is in 1748.

Levant Mine proper was launched in 1820, and its career was to last 110 years. The total value of the minerals it produced has been estimated as more than £2.25m. at contemporary values, thus placing it within Cornish mining's "top ten". Its output was mainly copper till the 1850s, but tin predominated after that. Although the Great Depression of the 1930s forced Levant to close at long last, its ore deposits - especially those far out under the sea - were still proving productive right up to 1991 as part of the expanded Geevor.

Reading a book like "The Mine under the Sea", written by Jack Penhale, a miner who began his working life in 1917 as a boy of 14, you cannot help noticing a sense of pride in having been part of "the Levant", as he calls it, and even a kind of affection for the old mine, in spite of the fact that the management was more reluctant than most to move with the times. Some innovations had, of course, been inevitable, since the workings extended an unprecedented distance under the sea bed, resulting in equally unprecedented problems. There were two vertical shafts connecting underwater levels, and it was necessary to haul ore up them. Almost unbelievably, in 1886 a steam whim engine and boiler were set up in a specially excavated cavern at the top of Old Submarine Shaft, 210 fathoms below adit, and "It worked despite the heat and smoke," says John Corin. A visitor the following year reported that the temperature there was usually 700°F. Compressed air, which had been in use for drilling since 1880, was a much better alternative: New Submarine Shaft was equipped with a compressed-air winding engine in 1897, and in 1901 the company invested heavily in a horizontal triple-expansion engine complete with flywheel weighing 20 tons, installed in the Power House. The availablity of high-pressure air in the further reaches of the mine helped to make

*The remains of Levant's Power House,
photographed in 1993.
In the distance, L to R:
arsenic stack and stamps-engine stack*

*working conditions more tolerable. (Jack Penhale describes a place
nicknamed "Little Hell" where the men "had to have a compressed air
supply to make ventilation and to lower the temperature by a degree or
two.") Little concern for working conditions was shown, however, when
the management decided in 1891 to use a steam locomotive for tramming
wagons underground, and when they abandoned this experiment this
was nothing to do with the noise, heat and stench but because the weak,
sharply-curving track and damp conditions created problems. A pit pony
was tried instead, with such success that a team of seven ponies came
into use - the only known example of ponies working underground in
Cornwall before World War I. An innovation which did prove beneficial
to all was the telephone system, installed in 1895.*

*In many other respects, though, the management's preference was to
stick to time-honoured methods and keep the old machinery going as
long as possible; and I suppose it could truthfully be said that the two
things for which Levant is best known today both result from that attitude.*

*The man engine had undoubtedly been a great boon to the miners for
many decades, but Levant persisted in using its man engine long after all
the others in the county had been abandoned or superseded. It seems
clear now that the horrific disaster of 20th October 1919, 62 years after
the machinery had been installed, was "just waiting to happen". With the
rod full of men ascending to "grass" at the end of the day shift, the wrought-*

iron cap on the Tee-bob at surface to which the rod was secured suddenly broke, and the rod fell unchecked. When it hit the bottom of the shaft it broke in two places and telescoped, crushing men and timberwork together and causing the loss of 31 lives. Track down John Penwith's little book if you can, and read "Death in the Afternoon."

Another piece of machinery that had a long life was a 24" (later enlarged to 27") cylinder steam engine made in about 1840 by Harvey's of Hayle and used to haul skips in a shaft on the cliff edge overlooking Levant Zawn. 90 years later it was still at work. Five years after the mine's closure it was saved from being scrapped, largely through the actions of J.H. Trounson. The Cornish Engines Preservation Committee was formed, and managed to raise enough money to buy it. It is now the oldest surviving beam engine in Cornwall. The Committee founded what is now called the Trevithick Society. Since 1966 the Levant Whim Engine has belonged to the National Trust, but the Trevithick Society has been very actively involved in the restoration of the old engine and associated equipment and buildings. The original plan to have the engine back in steam to celebrate its 150th birthday proved over-ambitious; instead, the great day was Good Friday 1993. Following that the engine has been in steam and open to the public during the season. For details of opening days and times, ring 01736-786156 or 01736-796993.

Centre: the Levant steam whim; right, the pumping-engine house
Photographed in 1996 by Simon Jones

WALK 8
BOSCASWELL, PENDEEN WATCH & PORTHERAS,
with a possible extension to MORVAH
Just over 3 miles, or about 5 miles if you include Morvah

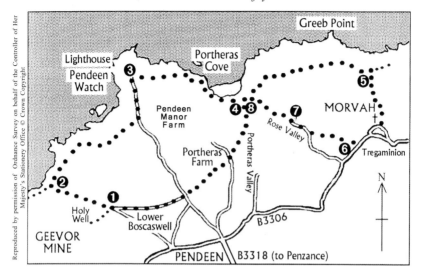

Although there are fewer mining remains on this walk than on others in this part of Cornwall, there is still plenty to interest the industrial archaeology enthusiast, especially in the Portheras valley. The coastal scenery is fine, of course, and Pendeen Lighthouse and Morvah church and village are further attractions. Guided tours of the lighthouse and engine room are available Monday to Friday from Easter to the end of September. The walk is fairly tough, with several steep and/or long climbs; the inland paths may possibly be rather overgrown, and there was mud in plenty, on the coast path as well as inland, when my wife and I last walked the route, in January 2004. Wellies strongly recommended. If you want food or drink along the way you will need to take them with you, although Pendeen Manor Farm (close to where the walk first joins the road to the lighthouse) was advertising cream teas during 2003-4.

The directions start at Lower Boscaswell. To drive there, take the road towards the coast from the B3306 at Pendeen: the Boscaswell Stores is at the corner where you turn. After about half a mile you will come to a small "square" where there is room for a few cars to park. A good alternative would be Pendeen Watch, where there is a fair amount of parking space near the lighthouse. If you decide to start there, pick up

99

the directions at point 3. A third possibility is the small car park at Lower Chypraze Farm above Portheras Cove. This is in the Rose Valley, at the seaward end of a minor road that leaves the B3306 just west of Morvah. For this, start following the directions just after the beginning of point 7.

First you might care to find the Boscaswell Holy Well. If so, take the track on the left, passing a long bungalow named Wheal Zandra. A little further on, the well is just round to the right beyond the last bungalow. A. Lane-Davies in *Holy Wells of Cornwall* says it is known locally as the Hesken ("sedge") Well, and an old lady told him it was "noted for horse leeches which ... were

frequently caught for medicinal use on cattle as well as human beings. ... They would never bite any but a diseased part. She spoke as if they knew the difference."

Return the same way.

1 **From the "square", follow the sign "To Coast Path". After passing the pretty little converted mission church and a few cottages, fork left along a track between hedges,** from which there is a good view to the left of the lower part of the Geevor Mine site and much of Levant. The green staining of the cliff is evidence of copper deposits. **Cross the stile beside a farm gate and walk straight on down the field.**

2 **At the bottom, officially you should cross the barbed-wire fence, scramble down the bank and turn right on the coast path, but until a proper stile is provided it is easier and safer simply to turn right and walk with the fence on your left.** On hazy or foggy days the experience of walking here tends to be dominated by deep booms issuing from a foghorn every 20 seconds or so, echoing eerily among the cliffs. **After the second kissing-gate comes a steepish climb up to Carn Ross.** On reaching the wooden stile at the top you have a good view of the source of that sound: the lighthouse at Pendeen Watch. The small stack on the skyline inland is part of an arsenic works at Trease, a relic of a short-lived attempt to reopen Boscaswell United Mine in 1907. **Soon you reach the valley leading down to Mill Zawn, where there are two small streams**

to cross, and as the path goes up on the far side it takes you beside what looks like evidence of mining: old walls beside the stream, which seems to have been diverted across a flat area, plus a pond and perhaps the remains of dumps. Tin streaming was undoubtedly once carried on in this valley, but the visible relics are of a series of small water-powered dressing floors, most of them probably dating from the 1870s, used by various mines including Pendeen Consols, Boscaswell Cliff and Boscaswell Downs. Such tin-processing works were often known as mills, and the name of the zawn may derive from that, although it is equally likely that there was a corn mill in the valley (compare Nanjizal or Mill Bay, Walks 3 & 4). **The coast path joins a road in front of a line of coastguards' cottages with a watchtower at the far end.**

Before turning left past them, you might care to accept the invitation, if it's still on offer, of a cream tea at Pendeen House (Pendeen Manor Farm). The attractive and historic house dates from the 15th century but was set on fire during the Civil War by Roundhead troops and was substantially rebuilt in the 1670s. In the farmyard is the entrance to Pendeen Vau, one of Cornwall's best fogous, underground passageways whose purpose is uncertain but was probably associated with primitive ritual. (The Explorer map indicates a fogou close to the recommended parking place at Lower Boscaswell, but little of it remains.) See Ian Cooke's *Mother and Sun* for very full details.

As you approach the lighthouse the view eastwards opens up as far as Carn Galver and Gurnard's Head.

Pendeen Lighthouse dates from 1900 and has a range of 28 miles. It was one of the last manned lighthouses in Cornwall.

3 Continue along the coast path. You soon reach a gate, on the right-hand side of which is a fenced shaft, with what appear to be ruined mine buildings above. These may be remains of Pendeen Consols, which had at least one pumping-engine house at or very near this site between 1853 and 1872. Before the lighthouse was built, the Pendeen Watch headland must have been dominated by mine buildings; if anything at all of them is left now, most of it is buried beneath the car park. The mine extended under the sea, where the richest deposits of tin, copper and lead were found to be. In its latter years Geevor extended its workings as far as this, and an underground road gave access to the old Pendeen sett, "just like a motorway". **Go down the steps on the left of the gate, and soon you are approaching Portheras** ("cove by ploughed land"). **Go down the cinder track. Rather than following the coast path sign straight away, you might care to go on down further to look at the Pendeen Fishing Station**, which is still in use (mainly potting for lobsters and handlining for mackerel) although many of the original buildings have gone or are derelict. The track leads past fishermen's sheds, the remains of pilchard cellars, to steep slipways and a rocky beach known as Boat Cove. **From there you could regain the coast path by a steep, narrow path. The coast path zigzags uphill; next comes a level stretch, usually very boggy; then the descent to Portheras Cove.**

4 Two streams rushing down steep little valleys meet just before flowing into the sea at the cove.

If you prefer to limit yourself to the shorter walk, omitting Morvah, don't go right down to the streams, but take the signed path up the first (Portheras) valley, picking up the directions at point 8.

Where the Rose and Portheras streams meet

If you want to do the full 5-mile walk you will now have to cross the combined waters - not an easy task after heavy rains, since there is no bridge. To find the easiest crossing place, follow the main path almost down to beach level, then cut back sharply to where there are some makeshift stepping stones; a rough path goes up quite steeply from there on the far side. (If you decide to spend time on the beach first, do please heed the warnings about "Razor sharp fragments" resulting from attempts to remove the carcase of the Polish ship *Alacrity*, wrecked here in 1963.) **Just after the sign warning about the danger to bathers there's a small cliff-edge path which leads to a good viewpoint, but from there you have either to return the same way or face a very steep, long climb up a rough path which in places near the top is somewhat overgrown with gorse. Better to keep to the official coast path, which curves right near the sign, goes up the valley for a few hundred yards and then is signposted sharp left.** Once you've climbed to the top of Carn Clough (a long, hard slog) you'll have no trouble in following the coast path, which keeps well inland of Chypraze and Tregaminion Cliffs, thus making for half a mile-or-so of what might be rather dull walking, but for the view ahead of the coast to Gurnard's Head, and inland of Watch Croft (crowned by the ruined engine house of Morvah Hill mine), Carn Galver and Zennor Hill. The two engine houses of Carn Galver Mine, beside the B3306, can also be seen. **Not far beyond a wooden stile beside what looks like a small sheepfold or shepherd's hut the path curves still further inland, and stepping-stones plus a stile take you across a marshy area and a stream, with Morvah church and hamlet visible on the right.** A few chunks of concrete the other side of the wall on the right just before you reach the stile seem to be all that's left of a pumphouse built over Morvah Holy Well; the many granite boulders round about are probably the remains of Tregaminion Chapel. (See section 6 for Tregaminion.)

5 **A few yards beyond the stream turn right.**

You might, however, care to go about a quarter of a mile further along the coast path (very rough and wet in places) first to see the ruined engine house of Morvah Consols, which stands beside the path. It was built in 1874 for a 24" engine, used for both pumping and stamping - but it worked only for a year. A rather flimsy fence surrounds the shaft. The winding at this mine was done by a horse whim, which was sited north-east of the engine house in an area now fenced off. The ruined building over there may be a remnant of the mine's smithy. Just west of the engine house is a walled yard containing substantial remains of dressing floors, including a large convex buddle, now grassed over but easily recognisable; and beside the yard on the west side is what looks like a dried-out mine pond. On the seaward side are many filled-in shafts and shallow pits.

The inland path - very muddy in places, thanks to cattle - brings you to Morvah church. The tiny village flanking it is dominated by Merthyr farmhouse. The low building on the left of that was - so the farmer and his wife told me - a blacksmith's shop; the large circular stone propped against it used to lie flat, and was used in the process of making the iron bands that went round the rims of wooden wheels. Notice also the tiny Board School building dated 1882, with a very ancient petrol pump outside. The school closed in 1937; in its latter years it had one teacher and about 50 pupils.

Morvah parish church

MORVAH

Morvah parish is one of the smallest in Cornwall, at least in terms of population: according to a note in the church there were "53 people in the parish at the last count."

The "churchtown" itself is tiny, but I was assured that 120 years ago, when the nearby mines were at their busiest, it was larger than Pendeen was then. Morvah Fair, held on the first Sunday in August, attracted large crowds in those days: a church document of 1850 refers to the "disorderly persons of every description" who assembled "for idle and profane amusement." Robert Hunt quotes a "Morva farmer" as saying, "A quarter of an acre would not hold the horses ridden to the fair, - the hedges being covered by the visitors, who drink and carouse as in former times. Morva Fair, however, is dying out." Morvah's present sleepiness is quite recent: the little lane that winds through it was the main road till 1940.

The name is unusually interesting, even though the old belief that it derived from the Breton word "Morverch" ("Sea-daughters", mermaids) is now discounted. In fact it apparently means "sea grave", and the farm at its centre is called Merthyr, "place with a saint's relics". Together the names would seem to amount to "saint's grave by the sea", but who was the saint? Not "St Morwetha" or "St Morveth", both of which are inventions derived from the word Morvah; not St Bridget or Briget of Sweden, to whom the church is dedicated: she died in Rome. Oliver Padel suggests it may have been the "Sanctus Morianus martyr" who according to William of Worcester (1478) was buried above the seashore west of Penzance. A church was built here in the 14th century, probably on the site of an

104

ancient Chapel of St Briget; the dedication to her has prompted considerable interest on the part of Swedish people, who have made several gifts to the church. Of the medieval building only the tower remains; the rest was demolished and rebuilt in 1828.

6 Walk past Merthyr farmhouse (that is, turn right on leaving the church). One of the cottages you pass once contained a cobbler's shop. **You now have a short stretch of the B3306 to walk along: please take great care, and walk facing the oncoming traffic, which can be quite heavy in summer.** The house you soon reach bears the name Tregaminion Manor: "the chief place, and almost the only one of note in this little parish," wrote Thomas Tonkin (1736). From Tudor times it belonged to the Lanyon family, from whom perhaps Lanyon Quoit is named - but Lanyon means "cold pool" or "cold stream", and the family may have taken its name from the place. **Opposite the post box there is a metal gate, with a not-very-obvious stile just past it. Cross that.** Cows had churned the area just beyond into a morass in January, but in summer it should be better. **Cross the field to a second stile, about 25 yards to the right of the corner, and continue in the same line to a third and fourth, the last of which is just to the right of a house called Wheal Rose.** (This was an alternative name for Carn Galver mine.)

7 Turn right on the minor road leading down to Rose Valley, which soon takes you past the car park at Lower Chypraze. The path from the farm crosses what looks like a leat and then runs for a while beside the stream. A little lower down, where the path is further from the stream, there are the remains of quite substantial old cornmill buildings. **Continue downhill to join the coast path above Portheras Cove, and cross the stream via the stepping stones, as before. (See point 4.)**

8 Part-way up the slope on the far side, leave the coast path by taking the signed inland path which heads up the Portheras Valley. The path is clear but narrow at first, with gorse and brambles threatening to grow over it; later it widens, and was extremely muddy in places in January. Before you have gone many yards you will see the ruins of quite large buildings down by the stream, and some of them are fairly accessible by means of side paths. The Archaeological Unit's survey has identified at least eight stamping-mill sites (often referred to as Oxman's Stamps) in this short valley.

WALK 8
THE PORTHERAS VALLEY

Some mining may have taken place in the valley, but its main historical interest results from the fact that nearby mines brought their tin here to be dressed. There were also corn mills, but most of them were in the Rose Valley. To satisfy the needs of all the stamping mills, supplementary supplies of water had to be taken from the Rose stream, by means of leats which ran at a high level around Chyrose Cliff (the seaward end of the steep hill that divides the two streams). Adam Sharpe argues that the need for this water to be returned to the corn mills in the lower part of the Rose Valley explains why so many of the stamping mills in the Portheras Valley had to be built on cramped sites at the upper end. The Archaeological Unit's survey found remains of eleven water-powered sites in the two valleys: three corn mills and eight stamps. Ten of them appear to have been in use - or at any rate their buildings were still in reasonable condition - during the 1870s, but of those all but two were derelict by 1908. The

eleventh was a small set of stamps erected in the mid-1920s near the mouth of the valley. How long that operated seems not to be on record. The Unit's analysis of the management of water power in these two valleys is among the most impressive things in its St Just publication. Mr Sharpe comments: "Almost all the buildings in these water-powered sites are in desperate need of conservation if they are not, within a few more decades, to disappear completely from the West Penwith landscape. That loss, were it to happen, would be tragic." I'm afraid nothing seems to have been done in the following 12 years, and all the structures look much more over-grown and inaccessible than when I first explored this fascinating place.

The remains of one of the many stamping works in the Portheras Valley

9 Just beyond two substantial ruins on the far side of the stream, you will see ahead a small stone bridge. Don't cross that, but take the muddy path on your right, which winds uphill. Cross the stile beside a metal gate and go on up to the farm buildings (Portheras Farm) via a path between hedges. Turn left at the farm; ignore the stile on the left as you leave the farmyard, but cross the one on the right about 50 yards later, then walk beside the wall on your left. The view to your left now includes the prominent pair of engine houses of Wheal Hearle or East Boscaswell - working period 1853-75 - which stand beside the B3318 road from Pendeen to Penzance; further right is the tower of Pendeen's 19th-century church, an interesting building modelled on the early cathedral at Iona. The hill between them and further off is Carn Kenidjack.

CARN KENIDJACK

Its nickname, "The Hooting Carn", is said to refer to eerie sounds made by the wind among the rocks. Legends about it abound, telling of howling demons and the Devil himself in the form of a ghostly horseman. In the 27 January 2004 issue of the "Western Morning News" Michael Williams tells of a friend who distinctly saw "people in white mackintoshes" at the top, who promptly disappeared. "HOOTING CARN FEARED AS A PLACE OF TERROR" reads the headline. If you want to brave the dangers yourself, there are plenty of paths to choose from - but don't go expecting the views of Cape Cornwall and Porthledden which illustrate the article, since they were apparently taken from Kenidjack Castle, on the coast!

Cross a stile on your left at the corner and another on your right just after that, so that now the hedge is on your right. Another stile and a boggy patch bring you to Calartha Farm. One more stile behind a small wooden gate and a path between hedges leads to a farm lane. Fork right, and then go straight on into Lower Boscaswell at the crossroads. To return to the suggested parking place keep right in the village, where the traditional miners' cottages are conveniently set opposite modern efforts for comparison.

WALK 9

CARN GALVER, PORTHMEOR, BOSIGRAN CASTLE & PORTHMOINA

A little over 4 miles, including the walk up Carn Galver (about 1½ miles),which could be omitted or done separately.
You should include the Carn Galver part of this route only in reasonably clear conditions, because it would be easy to get lost among the narrow, winding paths if you can't see far ahead.

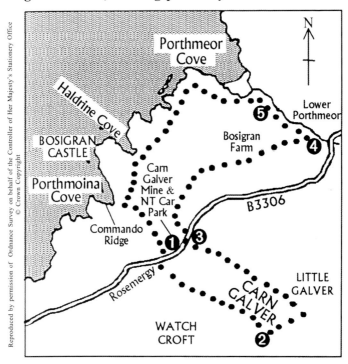

Scenically this is a very fine walk, with breathtaking cliffs cut by deep coves and zawns; two attractive short valleys; bare moorland littered with granite boulders, rising to one of the best-known and most beautiful tors in Penwith, from which in clear weather the view stretches from Zennor to the heart of the St Just mining district as well as inland to Ding Dong Mine. Even though the mines in this area were very insignificant compared with those near St Just, the principal mining remains hereabouts are exceptionally well preserved and accessible, thanks to the work of the National Trust. There is plenty of evidence of very early habitation, especially around the Carn, on Bosigran Cliff and at Porthmeor.

Of modern habitation, however, there is precious little - just three farms on or near the route - so once again you will have to take with you any provisions you may need. Good stout footwear is essential, both on Carn Galver and also on most of the coast path, and the field paths tend to be very muddy. In February 2004 this was more of a paddle and wade than a walk! The climb to the ridge of the Carn is fairly tough unless you are used to hill walking.

The National Trust's "Coast of Cornwall" leaflet No.10 is a very useful companion on this walk, especially in connection with the engine houses and the Porthmoina Tin Stamps. Its author, Des Hannigan, has also described a variation of the walk detailed here in *Wildlife Walkabouts*, particularly useful if you want information on the natural history and ecology of the area. Much of this route, extended to include Gurnard's Head, is described briefly but entertainingly by Gerald Priestland in *West of Hayle River*: he writes particularly vividly about the rock types and formations.

The directions are given from the small National Trust car park beside the engine houses of Carn Galver Mine, on the B3306 just east of Rosemergy.

CARN GALVER MINE

As is so often the way with particularly impressive or prominent engine houses, these are relics of a comparatively unsuccessful mine. Carn Galver, alias Wheal Rose or Rosemergy, is recorded as having produced 150 tons of tin in the 1860s and '70s. Both engine houses were built in 1871, so they had a short active life: the mine had closed by 1876. Carn Galver Mine's workings were drained by an adit about half a mile long leading into the engine (pumping) shaft, now filled, which lies adjacent to the half-fallen engine house. The adit's mouth can be seen at the back of Porthmoina Cove. Cyril Noall tells how a disaster similar to the later one at Wheal Owles (pages 79-80) was averted in 1867 as the new adit drew close to old workings containing "a vast body of water, say about 400 feet deep and near 1,000 feet long". An iron bar was driven some 4-6 feet ahead of the main excavation, and when this broke through to the "house of water" the miners had time to escape while the underground lake drained gently into the sea.

The photograph on pages 12-13 of the National Trust leaflet (also in several other publications) is excellent if you want to understand the various structures beside the car park. The tall stack was part of the

*Carn Galver Mine: the
pumping-engine house*

*pumping engine house, where a 30" beam engine drew water from a
780-feet-deep shaft on the seaward side; the more complete building was
for the 20" winding engine which drew "back to front" from the same
shaft, and the wheelpit built for the drum of the whim is still in good
order. There was a separate chimney, the base of which is not far from the
shaft; perhaps this stack was for the whim engine, but the NT leaflet
states it was earlier in date than these engine houses.*

1 Perhaps it's best to start with the Carn, while you've still got plenty of
energy! This part of the walk shouldn't take much more than an hour, or
90 minutes at the most, at the end of which you could return to your car
for refreshments. If you would prefer to do the coastal walk first, however,
set off along the road in the St Ives direction and start reading at the
second sentence in point 3 (page 113). **For the hill walk, go about 100**

yards along the road in the St Just direction towards the sizeable group of farm buildings, Rosemergy. Turn left at the public footpath sign. The path is pretty rough and in places soggy; here and there it seems to double as the bed of a stream. **Keep to the most obvious path, heading to the right of the hilltop, Carn Galver.**

CARN GALVER

The name, sometimes written as Carn or Cairn Galva, means "rock-pile of the look-out place": compare the nearby, slightly higher hill, Watch Croft. (An alternative explanation of the name, "Goats' Carn", is not mentioned by Padel. Compare "Geevor".) The highest point on the Carn Galver ridge (at the inland end) is 816 feet above sea level. A stone enclosure, probably as much as 5,000 years old, was identified on the slopes of Carn Galver by the Cornwall Archaeological Unit in 1984; it may have acted as a defensive wall for a group of wooden huts. In Cornish legend Cairn Galva is the home of the Giant Holiburn, "a very amiable and somewhat sociable gentleman," according to Robert Hunt. He (Holiburn, not Hunt!) ran a sort of protection racket, guarding the local human beings from the aggressive Trencrom giants in return for gifts of sheep and cattle. He married a farmer's daughter and begat "a very fine race", but his love of boisterous games with "human pigmies" led to an unfortunate incident when a playful tap on the head of a peasant "scattered his brains on the grass."

2 After about half a mile the path levels off and a low stone wall begins on the left; fork left there, and then take the side path starting at a gap in the wall, heading for the ridge now. There is, in fact, quite a number of fairly indistinct paths to choose among. I recommend that you aim for the highest outcrop, at the right-hand end of the ridge (rather oddly known as Little Galver), where it's worth scrambling up to the top for the excellent view south-east, dominated by the lonely engine house of Ding Dong mine (visited on Walk 10), with St Michael's Mount beyond, and the Lizard and Tregonning and Godolphin Hills in the far distance. You may be able to make out the engine house of Great Work mine on the left-hand slope of Tregonning. (Something we missed at the top of Carn Galver, probably because we were concentrating on the view, is a half-finished millstone. It's worth looking for, because the method used for splitting the granite, by making use of the fact that wood swells when it is wet, suggests that it was made before 1800.)

To continue the walk along the ridge towards the coast involves a lot of scrambling - sometimes over the top, more often just to left or right of it - but is very worthwhile for the beautiful rock shapes on the Carn and the ever-developing view of the flat coastal strip, created by marine erosion between one and four million years ago when it was covered by the sea, and the nearby hills such as Watch Croft to the left and Hannibal's Carn and Zennor Hill to the right, along with the Carn itself, were offshore islands. From the seaward end of the ridge you should be able to make out the church towers of Zennor, Pendeen and Morvah (the last quite close); Pendeen Lighthouse is prominent, and visible engine houses or stacks include those at Levant. The closest clifftop features are Commando Ridge and Bosigran Castle on either side of Porthmoina Cove; further right are Porthmeor Cove, Carn Gloose (Cornish, "grey rock") and a glimpse of Gurnard's Head. **Now your task is to follow the rather rambling and in places indistinct path among huge granite boulders down to the twin engine houses and former count house of Carn Galver Mine. If you manage to keep to the "official" path you should reach**

Coffee stop on the lower slope, looking west towards Rosemergy and Pendeen Lighthouse (January 1993)

the road opposite the count house, now adopted by the Climbers' Club of Great Britain, whose members find Commando Ridge and the Bosigran Main Face a particularly exciting challenge. Vivid photographs of climbers on these cliffs are included in yet another of Des Hannigan's publications, *Bosigran and the North Coast* (Climbers' Club Guides to West Penwith, 1991). The count house has associations with the poet and novelist D. H. Lawrence. Some details about his period of residence near Zennor during World War I are given on page 131. At that time the count house was let to the composer Philip Heseltine, better known as Peter Warlock. Lawrence and his German wife Frieda would occasionally visit for evening meals, and one night when they were there a flapping curtain at a lit window was interpreted by local patriots as signals to enemy submarines. However ludicrous this may seem now, it led directly to the Lawrences' being ordered to leave Cornwall late in 1917.

3 At the road turn right. The small ruined building on the right is said to have been the mine's gunpowder house and smithy, but if it was both at once I'm not surprised it's in ruins. **Just before the road bends, take the wide track on the left, cross the stile beside a metal gate, and turn right after about 100 yards, passing through a gap in a wall to join the "Church Path".** Sometimes still called "Church road", it is an ancient packhorse road which formed the link between all the settlements from St Ives to St Just until the existing road was built in the 17th century. **Nowadays much of it is badly maintained and hard to find, but for the first part you can't go far wrong if you head towards Bosigran Farm in a fairly straight line, keeping quite close to the hedge (wall) on the right most of the way. At the first field boundary there is a small gate for walkers beside the farm gate; after that you pass through several gaps in boundary walls before reaching the approach to the farm buildings. After the impressive granite stile there are two more small wooden gates as the path passes the big shed; then it runs between walls, and you cross another stile on the left, beside the second of two metal farm gates. Now continue in roughly the same direction as before; there's a confusing choice of possible paths, but watch out for a small chimney ahead, and head just inland of that. As the descent into the Porthmeor ("great cove") Valley begins, the official path (now very obvious, between walls) crosses two big stone stiles.** A spring just before the first stile creates boggy conditions at most times of year, but beyond the stile the water is channelled into what looks like a leat - perhaps to provide a water supply to the tinworks in the valley, although obviously the main Porthmeor or Porthmear stream was its principal power source. The farm ahead is Lower Porthmear; the Porthmear farms are the subject of an interesting chapter in *Three Hundred Years on Penwith Farms*.

4 Turn left immediately beyond the second stile, following the sign to the coast path. In winter, and probably even at other times unless the weather has been unusually dry, this beautiful valley is filled with the roar of water as it tumbles over rapids far below path level, and mostly hidden by thick vegetation.

The tin treatment plant is an excellent example, and perhaps the best place of any visited on walks in this book to illustrate the various processes. One writer states that it was used by Carn Galver Mine from about 1850, when the mine's needs outgrew the nearer tin-dressing complex at Porthmoina; according to another, it was used by Morvah Consols, a different enterprise: see page 103. Dressing floors like this may well have been run by independent companies who competed for business, like the smelting houses. The pit for the waterwheel that worked the stamps is near the top of the site; an old, rusty sluice gate can still be seen in the main leat that runs through the works; below are buddles and an old-style calciner with small stack still intact.

Part of the tinworks in the Porthmeor Valley

Just below the stack, on the left side of the path as you walk on down towards the sea, is a little stone chamber; Des Hannigan calls it a "field shelter ... which may be a relic of early settlement." Such little shelters, like the fishermen's huts at Priest's Cove (page 65), are called "crows" (pronounced to rhyme with "cows") in the St Just area. Further down the valley is a group of rectangular settling tanks. At least one corn or grist mill was powered by the Porthmeor stream, but which if any of the visible ruins are a relic of that I don't know. Since it was in use "pre-1800" according to the NT leaflet, all trace may well have gone now.

5 As you reach the cliff edge above the cove you may need to hunt around a little to pick up the coast path heading west (left). There is, in fact, another small NT sign on the far side of a little stream. The path runs about 15 yards inland from the cliff-edge fence and then crosses it by means of a wooden stile. There follows a very rough section, easy to stumble on, as you skirt "bald tor", Carn Moyle. Please don't stumble where the path runs disconcertingly close to a deep zawn, made the more fearsome by the blackness of the rock here. The next hilltop, and also the headland below it, give a fine view from Gurnard's Head to Pendeen lighthouse. Another zawn follows, and there's a stile to cross before you reach Halldrine Cove (the name possibly means "moor of thorn-bushes"). **A fairly stiff climb takes you to Bosigran Castle. The coast path goes well inland of it, but several side paths lead out to the headland and back.**

BOSIGRAN CASTLE

The name probably means "dwelling-house of the crane" - the bird, that is; as Des Hannigan mentions, the romantic notion that this was the site of the home of Ygrain, King Arthur's mother, has no basis in known fact. Mr Hannigan proposes "dwelling place in the dry valley" as an alternative explanation of "Bosigran", referring to the farm from which the headland is named. There is, of course, no "castle" here in the sense usually associated with the Knights of the Round Table: the promontory was a fortified settlement in Iron Age times, some 2,000 years ago. There seems to have been just one rampart across the wide neck of the headland. No trace has been found of dwellings within the "castle", but quite substantial remains of several courtyard houses from that period are nearby, and the headland may have been fortified as a possible refuge in case of emergency. The pattern of fields worked by Iron Age farmers still survives on this part of the coastal strip.

From Bosigran Castle there is a fine view of Porthmoina Cove, with its small waterfall. ("Porthmoina" sounds as if it ought to mean "little cove", in contrast to Porthmeor, but "moina" probably derives from a personal name.) Beyond is Commando Ridge, so called because it was used to train Marine Commandos during and for a few years after World War II.

The stream that creates the waterfall runs in a deep little canyon beside the fascinating remains of the Porthmoina Tin Stamps. Rosemary Robertson's reconstruction of this site (reproduced in the NT leaflet) is very helpful; in case you do not have it with you, I'll explain a few of the more important features. What looks like a gable end is in fact part of the wheelpit. Water was taken from the stream higher up the valley and conducted by a leat and launder to a large overshot waterwheel which drove the Cornish stamps machine, housed in a shed. (The tinners seem to have adapted an existing cornmill to their needs, and the gable end indicates the size of the original building.) The water from the wheel was then led to a series of rectangular buddles and settling tanks in which the stamped ore was washed. Cyril Noall's *The St Ives Mining District* includes details of the enlargement of "Bossigran Stamps" in 1860-1: a 36-foot

Porthmoina Valley: Part of the old grist mill, later adapted to house stamps

waterwheel with a new set of twelve heads of stamps plus two new patent Borlase's round buddles, 20 feet in diameter, were installed. Unlike the Porthmeor plant, this one does not seem to have had a calciner for burning off impurities such as arsenic before the tin was taken for smelting.

Incidentally, back in 1992 my wife and I caused much annoyance, as we wandered around the tinworks site, to a small flock of spectacular sheep grazing there (some can be seen in the photo), among which was a fearsome-looking ram with a pair of long straight horns in addition to the little curly ones sported by the ewes. We later learnt, from a rather battered NT notice, that these animals are a rare breed from the Isle of Man called Loughtons. I didn't see either sheep or notice when I was last there, in February 2004.

Follow the path up the valley, back to the car park. As you go you may notice the remains of several ponds (reservoirs to enable the tinworks to keep going in times of drought) and ruined structures (including what could be another wheelpit just below the first stile) which are evidence of older stamping mills. The various small hummocks and holes may be relics of early tin streaming and openwork mining. The largest pond, still full of water, is a little further west and not visible from this path - you will probably have noticed it from Carn Galver; the water in that one was used for the steam engines in the two consolidated engine houses.

Carn Galver as seen on the last part of the walk, with the whim-engine house on the left and the pumping-engine house on the right

WALK 10
MADRON & DING DONG MINE
A little over 6 miles

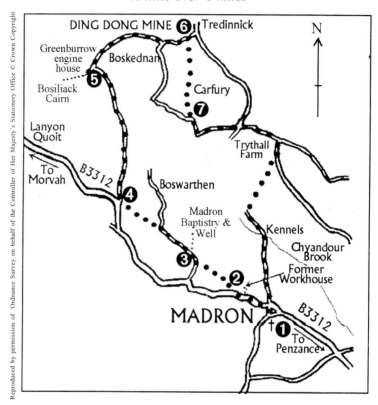

This inland walk is magnificent in very clear weather, when the panoramic views are unforgettable. The mine buildings are almost as impressive as their setting amidst the bare upland moors of Penwith, surrounded by evidence of prehistoric man and ringed by the far horizon; and to the industrial archaeologist they are of great interest both historically and technically.

The walk is based on the old village of Madron, which has a fine medieval church - a treasurehouse of beautiful and/or historically interesting objects - and many other attractive buildings.

A short diversion enables you to visit an ancient ruined chapel and nearby holy well. I must admit that I took the holy well on trust, because several days of teeming rain immediately before I first did this walk had made it inaccesslble to anyone not kitted out with wellies, and even in

January 2004, after an unusually dry autumn, despite much wading and squelching I failed to find it. Deep mud and miniature lakes made several of the paths shown on the OS maps, especially those around Trythall, virtually unusable; some of them also present such problems as badly-maintained stiles and blocked gateways, so I have not included them on the recommended route. There are quiet little country roads as alternatives to most of them, but not all, so unless you are planning your walk during a long drought I would strongly advise you to equip yourself with wellies.

Madron has a shop and a pub, but for the rest of the walk you are out in the wilds.

A much more detailed investigation of the mining remains at Ding Dong is featured in *Exploring Cornish Mines*, Volume 2.

MADRON

The name of the village is said to be derived from that of a Celtic saint called Maddern, about whom nothing is known, not even his or her gender. Charles Henderson stated in his notes written before 1924 that the word "Madron" is pronounced "Maddern", but it is rarely if ever heard in that form nowadays. A farm near the church was called Landithy, and this has led to speculation that an earlier saint called Dithy may have founded the first church here, but there seems to be little support from modern scholars for this theory. Landithy is mentioned by Henry Jennings (Vicar from 1922 to 1941) as the residence of the Knights of St John - presumably a lodging-house for pilgrims to the Holy Land. A Charter of King John in 1206 declared "the Church of St Madern de Runeri" (Runeri probably refers to Roseworthy in Gwinear) to be the property of the Knights of St John. Canon Jennings gives an interesting account of the origins and history of that body and its connection with the St John Ambulance Brigade.

Until 1867 Madron parish was one of the largest in the county, including the whole of Penzance and part of Newlyn, and it was only as recently as 1985 that Morvah parish was separated from Madron.

The church, like so many others in Cornwall, contains a few traces of a Norman building but is mostly from the 14th and 15th centuries, and was very heavily restored by J. P. St Aubyn in 1887 as well as by others since then. It is very spacious and has an exceptionally fine collection of monuments including the impressive slate memorial to the son of the first Mayor of Penzance, John Maddern (died 1621) - whose surname, I

presume, was derived from his family's parish. An inscribed stone, probably of the 6th or 7th century, discovered in 1936 under nine layers of plaster, is now clearly visible beneath a stained-glass window in the south west corner. Another object of special note is a panel of ten angels carved in alabaster, probably from the 14th century; this is on the south wall of the Lady Chapel. Notice also the medieval bench-ends in the Chapel, and the carved roof bosses. Among the best-known exhibits in the church is the Nelson Banner, which was made in 1805 to celebrate the victory at Trafalgar as well as to mourn the Admiral's death: Penzance fishermen had been the first to report the news in England. The banner is in a glass case near the north door. On all sides there are well-labelled relics and photographs of the church before restoration, and the excellent guidebook available in the church lists and describes most of them. Of special interest (I trust!) to readers of this book is the "Ding Dong Bell", which like the banner and the Maddern tablet is near the north door. A notice states that it was "last rung in 1878 to bring up the final shift of miners". In a display case are "tin marks" used in the parish since the 12th century.

In the churchyard are two ancient crosses. The larger one, with a carving of Jesus, stands close to the tower; the holes in the base (and possibly also those in the cross itself?) were, says Andrew Lanyon, made by local apprentices practising drilling with hand tools. The other, with a Gothic cross carved on it, is beside the path leading to the south door.

Canon Jennings' history of the parish has a particularly detailed and fascinating chapter on the administration of the poor law in Madron, and "Madron's Story" paints a grim picture of conditions for the unfortunate inmates. It was at Madron Workhouse (the remains of which can still be seen, as mentioned in the directions) that the St Ives rag-and-bone merchant and "primitive" artist Alfred Wallis died in 1942, despite the celebrity his work had already begun to achieve through the patronage of Ben Nicholson, Barbara Hepworth and others. They paid for his funeral, though, and he is buried at Barnoon cemetery in St Ives. Final closure of the workhouse came as late as 1951.

There is a small public car park beside the lych-gate of Madron church. To drive to that, turn left as you enter the village, coming from the Penzance/Heamoor direction. Notice beside the church the village school, the subject of an excellent publication by the local WI in 1978. It was founded early in the 18th century by George Daniel, the son of Alexander Daniel, whose tomb bears an epitaph which is quoted in all the guide books. Just to be different, I'll leave you to find it for yourself. It's in the graveyard, near the south door of the church.

1 **From the main entrance to the church, on the north side, walk along the road straight ahead, passing on your left the Thomas Simon Bolitho Institute and Landithy Hall** (the village hall and community rooms, with cottages in the same style on either side; they date from 1909). For the Bolitho family, see *A View from Trencrom*, page 9. **The William IV ("Circa 1700") is on your right at the corner. There turn left along Fore Street, past the post office/stores** - the odd-shaped building opposite, now a garage, was the blacksmith's shop - **and continue for about a quarter of a mile,** passing the Madron Methodist Church and the overflow graveyard.

A very short diversion to the end of the road on the right (called Mount View, though the sign saying so had disappeared by 2004; the road in question comes a few yards before Parc Abnac) will bring you to the abbatoir, the Madron Meat Co., which occupies parts of the remains of the old Madron Workhouse - the "gaunt" building whose "ashy walls" Jane Tregenza passed on her way to Madron Well. "She shivered as she passed, and was sad, knowing that a whole world of poverty, failure, sorrow, regret, lay hidden in that cold, still pile." (Eden Phillpotts: *Lying Prophets*, 1897) The workhouse itself was given the name Mount View in 1916 - a cruel irony, since the windows were "inserted so high that even a giraffe would have had difficulty to look through them." (Quoted from *Madron's Story*, which includes a good photograph of the workhouse as it was.) **Return the same way to the main road and continue as before.**

2 Cross the stile beside the last house on the right and walk with the hedge on your right. After two stiles the path runs between hedges and comes to a minor road. Already you have a view ahead of two of the three surviving engine houses of Ding Dong; the tall hill furthest to the right is Castle-an-Dinas, recognisable by the large quarry near the top and the folly known as Rogers' Tower above it. (See Walk 1 in *A View from Trencrom.*)

3 Turn right on the road.

For the short diversion to Madron Baptistry and Wishing Well, turn right again immediately on to a track, and then take the path on the left after a few yards. The path is almost sure to be muddy, and in fact parts of it double as a small stream in winter. After about a quarter of a mile, hundreds of assorted rags tied to low branches plus a sign pointing left indicate the proximity of the Well; if you succeed in finding it, congratulations. The way ahead to the Baptistry was clear, however, and it's a delightful spot, a beautiful little paved chapel, complete with altar, and a font supplied with flowing water. An explanatory notice nearby has been sadly vandalised and is now totally illegible.

MADRON BAPTISTRY AND WELL

The site of the tiny chapel may have been the spot chosen by St Maddern for his oratory - and perhaps before him by St Dithy. The ruins there now are, of course, much later in date, although the lower parts are claimed to be pre-Norman. The "font" inside it, and also the "wishing well" about a hundred yards away, have always been credited with great powers of healing. The miraculous cure of the crippled John Trelille in about 1640 was told in detail by Bishop Hall of Exeter a few years later, and there are many accounts of mothers bathing their children in the water and performing other rituals. The separate well may once have been enclosed

The altar in the Baptistry

in a well-house, and Charles Henderson states that there were formerly steps leading down to the well, but there is no sign of any of that now, and indeed many changes have been made to chapel, well and stream over the centuries. For example, the well-water was, according to the church guidebook, "the main supply to Penzance up to 1830" , and much more recently it was still being "piped down to Madron as a domestic water supply"(Leggatt). Some of the pipework is still visible. A leat carrying the water ran beside the parish church until the churchyard was extended during the 1820s. The custom that pilgrims should tie a piece of cloth to a twig near the well as proof of their visit or as an offering to the saint is very ancient; according to Quiller-Couch it is done in many countries to protect cattle, propitiate the fairies or stave off the sorcery of the Druids. This mixture of Christian and pagan belief is well captured by Joan Tregenza in the Eden Phillpotts novel quoted earlier. Speaking of the rags "tored off a petticoat, or some sich thing" by mothers after dipping their babies naked in the brook, she says, "They hanged 'em up around about on the thorn bushes, to shaw as they'd 'a' done more for the good saint if they'd had the power. An' theer's another marvellous thing as washin' in thicky waters done: it kep' the fairies off - the bad fairies I mean, 'cause there'm good an' bad piskies, same as good an' bad men folks."

To continue the walk, return the same way and turn right on reaching the road. Before long there is an old wayside cross beside the road, probably set up here as a guide for pilgrims seeking the holy well. An old tradition is that if you walk three times round it and spit each time, the devil can't get you. **Where the road bears right to Boswarthen Farm, continue ahead on the surfaced path, which will eventually bring you to a stile splashed with orange paint. From there go straight on across the field** (but pause a moment and look back at the superb view of Mount's Bay, with the Goonhilly Satellite Earth Station dishes visible on the skyline way beyond the Mount) **to a stile on the left of a gateway. The path continues straight ahead, crossing four more stiles, two of which are becoming rather festooned with brambles. The last stile brings you to the main Madron - Morvah road.**

4 Fork right immediately on to a minor road. As this gradually climbs towards Ding Dong it gives you a view to the left of Lanyon Quoit (though you may have trouble finding it, since it is half a mile away and below the skyline), and almost behind you, with the sea horizon beyond it, can be seen the tall tower of St Buryan church. **After passing the entrance to Bosiliack Farm the road dwindles to a rough track, which soon brings you to the beautiful Greenburrow Shaft engine house of Ding Dong Mine.** From that the view is even more panoramic - one of the finest in Cornwall, in fact - and includes the rocky tor of Carn Galver (see Walk 9), the rounder Watch Croft on its left, and the ancient settlement of Chun Castle further left again.

Well within a mile of this spot are the famous ancient monuments known as the Men an Tol (holed stone), the Men Scryfa (inscribed stone) and the Nine Maidens (the Boskednan stone circle) and the OS maps indicate what looks a simple little circular route on paths that would include all three. I don't advise you to try it, however, unless you are equipped with wellies, gorse-proof trousers, a compass, a large-scale map and advanced orienteering skills. No doubt I am exaggerating the problem, but I wasted an hour trying to decide among several dozen equally likely-looking little paths, all of which ended in bogs or impenetrable gorse or both! Ian Cooke's books and booklets are excellent guides to these sites, so if you're keen to see them I'll leave you in his capable hands.

Let's take a look at the engine house and its immediate surroundings now. This best-known of the three recognisable engine houses on the site was built in 1865 for a 40" engine which pumped from the 480-feet-deep shaft it stands beside as well as from Ding Dong Shaft, several hundred yards to the north-east, by means of flat-rods. (The engine used at Greenburrow had worked at Ding Dong Shaft until 1865.) Twice this century the dumps of mine waste around the building have been sifted for the residues of metals they contain; quite recently Geevor Mine applied to work them over again, but local environmentalists objected and permission was denied. Notice the large, masonry-lined balance pit beside the shaft. The engine house was consolidated in the late 1980s under the Manpower Services scheme.

The balance pit beside Greenburrow Shaft

DING DONG MINE

This is reputedly one of the oldest mines in Cornwall. Dines mentions the claim that some of its lodes were discovered "in distant, possibly in pre-historic, times," and the legend that Jesus Christ visited Cornwall sometimes includes Ding Dong Mine on the itinerary. To Cornish engineers, Ding Dong is best known for the 28"-cylinder inverted engine designed by Edward ("Ned") Bull, which was put up at Ding Dong Shaft in 1796, and which infringed James Watt's Patent. Watt sent his lawyers who nailed an injunction on the engine-house door, following which Richard Trevithick altered Bull's engine to exhaust to atmosphere.

The mine's main active period began in 1814. By 1850 it was employing about a hundred people. By 1874 it had five beam engines and a work force of 273, but there was little tin ore left, and when prices fell to £41 per ton in 1877 the decision was taken to close. During the following months an effort was made to re-open it, but the re-constituted company was finally dissolved in 1880. Unsuccessful attempts to re-work the mine were made in 1912 and 1928.

Its name, which took the form of "Dindods" in the 13th century, has led to a good deal of speculation. As well as another Ding Dong mine near Gunnislake on the Devon-Cornwall border, there were Bal Ding in

Wendron parish, Wheal Ding near Lanivet and Ting Tang Mine near St Day. Canon Jennings mentions the suggestion that "Ding Dong" means "head of the lode", referring to an outcrop of tin on the hill. The "Ding Dong bell" displayed in Madron church is, of course, much more modern than the name.

5 Before continuing the main walk, you might care to walk a little way along the track that runs westwards from the engine house (starting at the open gateway with what looks like a sawn-off telegraph pole laid across). This diversion provides a good view of several deep pits, open shafts, and so on, left by the miners. A good many shafts at Ding Dong lurk unsuspected and unprotected among the gorse and bracken so it is important not to wander off the recognised paths. (Further over to the left is

The Greenburrow engine house

a well preserved and impressive ancient monument, the Bosiliack Chambered Cairn; unfortunately it is on private ground and not visible from the footpath. The aerial photos on page 174-5 of *Exploring Cornish Mines* Volume 2 clearly show the Cairn and the mine workings.) **Take the same way back to the engine house.**

Return to the main track by which you came up from Madron and turn left on it. It curves right and heads north-east through an area where reminders of the mine are visible almost everywhere. On the left are several fenced shafts, and half-hidden by the scrub covering the rough ground on the right are old walls surviving from the dressing floors, among them the foundations of a stamps engine house (24"-cylinder engine) and part of the embankment which carried a tramway from the Tredinnick Shaft at the eastern end of the mine to the battery of 40 or possibly 44 stamps. Where the track curves right, a metal farm gate on the right marks the entrance to the site of a whim-engine house, now gone. Not far beyond that is the 480-feet-deep Ding Dong Shaft, the one which was linked by flat-rods to the Greenburrow engine.

Quite close to the small group of houses are two shafts: Hard Shaft on the right of the track and Ishmael's on the left. In 1868 the mine decided to drain Ishmael's, which had been flooded below the 70-foot level for at least 20 years. Two men who went down to fit siphons were badly scalded in an explosion, and soon afterwards the mine manager and four other miners had similar experiences. When Davy lamps were taken down the shaft it was found that the problem resulted from fire damp (methane gas) caused by the timbers which had lain rotting for so long. Though a well-known hazard in coal mines, fire damp was one of the few dangers not normally faced by Cornish miners.

The engine house (right, with Mount's Bay in the distance) held a whim engine, probably 25"; the masonry wall beside it shows where the whim drum was mounted, and the fact that it lines up with the Tredinnick (or Tredinneck - the name means "gorse farm") Shaft, beside the third engine house, indicates that it hauled from that one.

Go on down the road now (that is, walk on in roughly the same direction) to visit the Tredinnick engine house, whose engine, a short-stroke 30", pumped not only from Tredinnick Shaft - the deepest in the mine at 135 fathoms - but also from Providence Shaft (110 fathoms) about 150 yards to the west, by means of flat-rods. The engine house, built about 1830, is said to have used some granite taken from the "Nine Maidens" stone circle, which despite its name probably originally had nineteen stones, eight of which are no longer *in situ*.

To continue the walk, carry on down the road past several houses.

6 Turn right along the short lane which starts just before a house named Chynoweth - there is a wooden garage on the right at the start of the lane - and cross the big stone stile on your left almost at the end of the lane. Now walk with the hedge on your left, cross a second stile beside an open gateway and continue in the same direction through a second gap and over another big stone stile. The path now runs on the left side of a hedge, passes through the second gateway on the right and then goes diagonally across a field towards the right-hand building in the small hamlet of Carfury. Cross the stile, go through the yard and turn left along the road.

7 At the junction, where there is a small flooded quarry on the right, turn left. At the crossroads go straight on. Notice the quite large quarry over to the left, in line with the much bigger one at Castle-an-Dinas. Follow the main road round to the right, signed to Heamoor and Penzance, and where there is a left bend go straight on along a bridleway between hedges. (In January 2004 this was even wetter and muddier than the path to Madron Baptistry, thanks mainly to the horses: definitely wellie territory!) Where you reach a wider path continue ahead, downhill. The path becomes quite narrow again and rather rough underfoot as it descends more steeply into the Chyandour valley. After a few hundred yards on a lane you will reach Kennels Cottage, which takes its name from the fact that the Western Hunt has its headquarters close by. Cross the bridge over the stream and walk up Aldreath road into Madron. A stile on the left near the top of the hill enables you to walk on a footpath which runs beside the road (on the far side of the tall hedge) and gives you a fine view over Mount's Bay. The path continues over several more stiles. On reaching a small housing estate, take the first right turning. At the road, turn left, then at Madron Post Office left again and right to return to the parking place beside the church.

WALK 11
ZENNOR, GURNARD'S HEAD AND ZENNOR HEAD
A little over 5 miles, or about 6 if you include Treen.
Round walks of about 1½ and 3 miles are also described.

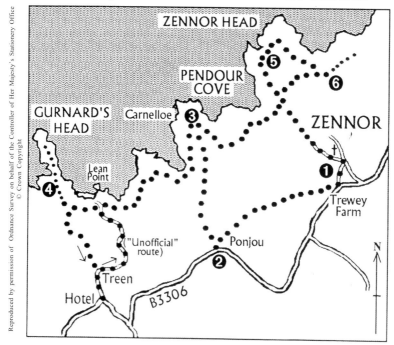

The Zennor area had comparatively few mines, but there are some unusually interesting sites for the industrial archaeologist on these routes. At Carnelloe are the clifftop remains of a small mine which relied on water power: two big wheelpits have survived, and the layout of the surface workings of this mine is exceptionally easy to interpret. The ruined engine house of Gurnard's Head Mine is among the most spectacularly-situated of any visited on walks in this book. The Wayside Museum in Zennor has a very well-presented collection of artefacts related not only to mining but also to agriculture and dozens of other rural trades and crafts. I hardly need to point out the magnificence of the scenery on the coastal parts of this walk - more accurately, "these walks", since there is a choice of routes to suit most tastes and abilities. The coast path between Zennor Head and Gurnard's Head is quite tough walking, so don't be deceived by the fairly short distances involved.

The pub in Zennor has a name which implies that mining in these parts was once rather more important than I suggested at the start of this note. The food available there is reputedly very good. There are seasonal toilets at the car park in the village. The pub at Treen, near Gurnard's Head (strictly speaking a hotel, but it has a pub "feel"), has long been known for its imaginative menus; it is open every day from midday for full meals (last orders 9.15pm), teas and other light refreshments.

The book to read in connection with this walk and No.12 is Alison Symons' *Tremedda Days*: see Further Reading.

Directions start at the car park beside a disused chapel a few yards beyond the Wayside Museum in Zennor. The village is signposted from the B3306 about 5 miles west of St Ives.

ZENNOR

The village takes its name from a saint called Sinar, Sinara or Senara, unknown elsewhere. Most references suggest that the saint was female, and some scholars believe she may be the Breton princess Azenor or Asenora, mother of St Budock.

The church's history follows the pattern familiar in Cornwall: a Celtic foundation (probably around 700 AD) whose church was probably mainly of timber; a stone building of the Norman period, much enlarged in the 14th and 15th centuries and heavily restored in the 19th. Old photographs near the organ show something of what the interior looked like before 1890, with box pews and a gallery.

The colour guide on sale in the church is attractive and lively but contains little detailed information; it does, however, include the legend of the mermaid and Matthew Trewhella, so I'll leave you to read it there or in one of the many books on Cornish legends and folklore. A small notice beside the so-called Mermaid Chair near the pulpit explains the Christian significance of "a mermaid in Church". The carving of the mermaid, "with a comb and a glass in her hand", was originally a bench-end.

Under the tower, where the bell ropes are, one of the old slate gravestones commemorates Matthew Thomas, killed in 1809 by a fall of ground at "Wheal Chance on Trewey Downs", an old mine whose workings were close to those of the restored Rosevale Mine, south-east of the village. A grave-stone outside tells a very different story: Matthew Hollow died at 95, his wife Elizabeth Botterell at 100, and their daughter Elizabeth Uren at 105; Matthew was born in 1816 and his daughter lived till 1949.

The sundial on the tower, dating from 1737, was made by Paul Quick, a relative of one of Zennor's best-known figures, the poet (purists say "rhymester") Henry or Henny Quick. The bicentenary of his birth occurred recently. You can read his verse autobiography in "The Life and Progress of Henry Quick of Zennor", edited by P.A.S. Pool (Truran, 1984).

> "My printed copies then did sell, / And people seem'd to like them well; / Parish to parish, town to town, / I travelled through and sold them round. / ... Please to take pity on poor Henny, / I love to gain an honest penny."

The Tinners Arms may have suggested The Tinners' Rest in D. H. Lawrence's story "Samson and Delilah", which tells of a miner who returns from the USA to claim back the wife and daughter he had deserted sixteen years before; the setting of the pub in the story seems to be Pendeen, but Lawrence is said to have written it while staying at the Tinners Arms early in 1916. If you want to go in search of the cottage Lawrence and Frieda later rented, take the path signposted to St Ives (the "Church Road"), on the right just behind the church. After nearly a mile this reaches Tregerthen farm; a minor road to the right from there leads to Higher Tregerthen, where the cottage is. Next door is the "Tower", where Katherine Mansfield and John Middleton Murry lived for a while at the same period. The interesting map in Jean Nankervis' book would be useful in exploring that area. See the comments on Carn Galver Mine's count house (page 113 in Walk 9) for further details on this topic.

THE WAYSIDE MUSEUM

The little "folk museum" at Zennor was a very simple and almost primitive affair forty years ago when I first saw it, despite having been in existence for nearly thirty years even then. During the last decade the buildings have been extensively renovated and the collection has been restored where necessary and greatly enlarged. Most of it is housed in various outbuildings including the Trewey watermill at the end of the garden, where much of the old machinery is still in place. The cottage (originally the miller's house) also contains displays in the kitchen, with its original open fireplace. Other items, including two small waterwheels, are in the open air. "The theme of the Museum," says the excellent Souvenir Guide, " is life in Zennor from 3000 BC to the 1930's." The mining relics include the two waterwheels and also an early set of stamps. One complete room is devoted to a display of pictures, tools and mineral specimens associated with local mining and quarrying. The collection of large-scale maps of the Zennor area, prepared in 1985 for the National Trust, will also be an attraction for walkers, especially if they want to know more about the ancient archaeology of this district.

Music lovers may like to know that the Cornish composer George Lloyd, whose works are enjoyed especially by those who do not normally like "modern" music, wrote his opera "Iernin" while living at the mill house, shortly before the Museum was started.

Light refreshments are available, and the shop sells gifts and books. Opening times in recent years have been daily from 10am between Easter and the end of October. For up-to-date information phone 01736-796945.

1 **For the shortest walk - a circular tour of Zennor Head - turn left, walk between the church and the pub and take the minor road on your left - there is a footpath sign to Zennor Head. After nearly half a mile you will pass the substantial modern bungalow called Carn Cobba, and then you soon reach the coast path. Continue straight ahead for the headland, picking up the directions at point 5.**

For the main walk, turn right on leaving the car park, walk back past the Wayside Museum to Trewey Farm, at the main road, and there take the signposted public footpath on the right. For a few yards you are on a farm track - muddy in winter - and then you cross the first of several "stiles" that might better be called granite cattle-grids. ("Cornish stiles", they are called in these parts.) **The grassy path runs**

between hedges at first, then follows the hedge on the right. The course of the path is mostly clear, heading in a fairly straight line towards the rocky ridge of Carn Galver. The seventh stile (just in case you've been counting) is beside a gateway at the corner of a field; the path then runs beside a hedge on the right, and after one more stile joins a track which crosses a stream and runs beside a group of cottages at Ponjou, "bridges".

2 Just before the track reaches the main road, turn right on to another track heading for the coast. (There is a public footpath sign beside the road.) Keep to the main track as it curves right, and cross the little breeze-block stile next to a wooden farm gate beside the stream. At this point you get your first good view of Gurnard's Head, but don't let that distract you from noticing the big wheelpit down on the left as you approach the bungalow. All around you now are relics of a small mine called Carnelloe or Zennor Consols.

The upper wheelpit at Carnelloe

CARNELLOE MINE OR ZENNOR CONSOLS

Zennor Consols was a group formed in 1851, "consolidating" several old mines including Zennor Head Mine and Carnelloe (sometimes spelt "Carnella" or "Carnellow"). There are records of work in progress at Carnelloe in 1862, when the mine apparently depended completely on water power. A 42-ft. waterwheel was used for winding and to drive twelve heads of stamps. Another company took over in 1872 and sank a new shaft named Engine Shaft. That might seem to imply the use of steam, but it was the normal name in Cornwall for any shaft containing pitwork, however it was driven: steam, horse or water. A "water engine" rather than a "fire engine" was used here: the new company bought a 37-ft. waterwheel for pumping and an iron waterwheel to drive eight heads of stamps and also haul up a tramway attached to the face of the cliff. The mine closed in 1876 despite very optimistic assessments by miners of its prospects. The only recorded output is 6 tons of black tin in 1872-3. Justin Brooke, who supplied several of the foregoing details, also told me that an ambitious plan to re-open Carnelloe Mine as recently as 1964 was abandoned only for legal reasons.

Back in 1993 I had a long chat with the owner of the bungalow, and promised him I would stress that all these relics are on private land. Most of them can be seen quite well from the paths, and there is no reason to go clambering about on and among them - an activity which has caused considerable damage to some features as well as being distinctly risky. The bungalow itself is a relic of the mine, since it was used as its count house - and I was told there have even been some passers-by who have roamed around the building peering through the windows! The owner told me that the original workings of the mine were on the higher ground inland (the OS Explorer map indicates "Shafts" a short way east of Carnelloe), and he believes that the earliest dressing floors were up there. (Dines identifies these inland workings as probably those of a small mine called Wheal Dollar; this was working with Carnelloe during the 1830s.) Later, a reservoir was built nearer the cliffs - one wall of it can be seen up on your right just above the upper wheelpit - and water to power the two big wheels was brought to it by a leat from the stream you have just crossed. The first waterwheel did two jobs: it wound from the shaft down by the cliff-edge, hauling the tin-stuff up to this level by means of a short tramway, and it operated the stamps. Hidden by the low scrub on the right of the wheelpit are small dressing floors including buddles. Justin Brooke tells me that a slag-heap was found nearby, suggesting that the mine also had its own blowing house (for smelting) at one period. According to *Tremedda Days* the smelting works was on the east side of Carnelloe headland, and the crushed and buddled ore was taken there in panniers or donkey-carts.

Continue down the path, which runs to the right of the bungalow

(what a superb view, in both directions!) and then steeply down to join the coast path.

3 Here turn right, picking up the directions at point 4, if you prefer not to include the diversion to Gurnard's Head - but first it would be worth going a few yards left to see other features of Carnelloe mine. **For Gurnard's Head turn left, past the lower wheelpit**. This is surrounded by several gunnises (surface workings); the shaft from which the waterwheel pumped, now choked at surface, is, I understand, on the seaward side of the wheelpit. **The path approaching the stream, which ends as a waterfall at Porthglaze Cove, is steep, wet and rather rough in places, but beyond the footbridge things improve.** This stretch of coast, called Boswednack Cliff, is National Trust property, as is Gurnard's Head. Look back to get a clear view of one of the stopes beside the lower wheelpit. Near the tip of the closest headland, Carn Nean Point, are, I'm told, the remains of a horse-whim plat which was employed, along with a 30" beam engine for pumping from two shafts, by a mine called North United during the 1840s. Rather strangely, there seem to be no traces of mine dumps in that area. **Soon comes another bridge over a rushing stream,** and presumably this one supplied power to the nearby Gurnard's Head Mine, in addition to the steam engine it invested in for pumping. **The coast path crosses a wider track and continues ahead, up beside the engine house,** the bob wall of which is perched precariously on the lip of an open shaft. Down beside the edge of the cliff is a ruined building, a relic of the Gurnard's Head pilchard seining fishery. The engraving of its wooden landing stage beneath the sheer cliffs at Treen Cove comes

from I.T. Tregellas' snappily titled *Peeps into the Haunts and Homes of the Rural Population of Cornwall* (1879).

GURNARD'S HEAD MINE

Above: probably about 1890, over 40 years after the mine closed.
Below: As it was a century later. Remains of the stack on the right,
Treen Cove and Carnelloe Point in the distance.

The earliest recorded mining venture here was the Treen Copper Mine,
which started before 1821 and had sunk its main shaft on a small rocky
headland where a ten-foot-high wall was required to keep the sea out at
spring high tides. By 1837, when the name Gurnard's or Gurnett's Head
Mine was in use, the main shaft had reached a depth of nearly 250 feet

below sea level, and there is evidence that the mine was still relying entirely on water power then. A 40ft. waterwheel was being used for pumping at that time. Collins states that it employed 24 people then. A new company took over in 1843, but this lasted only till 1847, despite some good finds of copper. The engine house, built for a 30" pumping engine, apparently belongs to this period.

Having come this far it would be a pity not to extend the walk to Gurnard's Head itself, from which the views are magnificent. On the right side of the coast path about a quarter of a mile beyond the engine house - just before quite a steep climb - are the foundations of what the OS map calls Chapel Jane.

CHAPEL JANE

An excavation carried out here in 1964-6 was the subject of an interesting article in "Cornish Archaeology" No. 7 (1968). The authors, Vivien Russell and P.A.S. Pool, concluded that this little building probably was indeed a chapel, likely to have been used between about 1100 and 1500. Among the objects found was a "mensa" or altar table, rather similar to the one at Madron Baptistry (Walk 10), upon which the priest would probably have placed a portable altar. Nearby is or was a Holy Well credited with great healing powers, but the exact site of that is very doubtful; it may have been destroyed by cliff erosion. There is in fact a small natural spring some 18 feet to the south, just below the cliff edge. The name "Chapel Jane" was supposed to have been first used by the early-18th-century historian William Hals, who explained it as meaning "narrow chapel". That is certainly apt, but Russell and Pool believe Hals actually wrote "Idne" or "Jelne", and that he intended "Chapel Innyall" or "Ynyal", which as mentioned elsewhere may have been an old name for Gurnard's Head. A document of 1580 referred to the building as "Innyall Chapel". Dr C.A. Ralegh Radford has suggested that that it may have been built here to serve the needs of the fishermen based at Treen Cove: not just their spiritual needs (prayers for good catches, safe return, and so on), but also their physical safety, since there is some evidence of a small tower at the western end of the building where a guiding light may have been placed.

4 **Not far past that, fork right for the headland.**

GURNARD'S HEAD

Its modern name is said to allude to the supposed resemblance of the promontory to the fish; a century or more ago the normal version was "Gurnett's Head", "gurnet" being an alternative name for a gurnard. Its old name is Izner, possibly derived from Cornish ynyal ("wild, desolate"), and the maps also label it Trereen Dinas, from Cornish tre-dyn dynas, "farm of the fort fort". (The "farm of the fort" is, of course, Treen; there is another Treen in Penwith, and that stands beside a headland called Treryn Dinas: see Walk 2.)

Like almost every other high Cornish headland, this one was fortified during the Iron Age. Two ramparts and three ditches can still be traced across the neck; the inner wall is of masonry and seems to be equipped with three steps from which the defenders could aim their slingshots. Archaeologists in 1939 detected the foundations of 16 round houses, each about 20-30 feet in diameter. All these remains are thought to date from about 200 BC.

Francis Kilvert's diary describes a visit to Gurnard's Head in 1870:"I wandered round the cliffs to the broken rocks at the furthest point of the Head, and sat alone amongst the wilderness of broken shattered tumbled cliffs, listening to the booming and breaking of the waves below and watching the flying skirts of the showers of spray. Perfect solitude."

Eventually return to Carnelloe by the same route (picking up the directions five paragraphs on), unless you want to include the following diversion, which would add about a mile to the walk.

From Gurnard's Head there is a path inland to the hamlet of Treen, where you could get refreshments at the Gurnard's Head Hotel. For that, return along the same path at first, but don't fork left, and when you reach the coast path continue straight ahead uphill, through bracken. Keep to the main path as it winds up to the top of the hill; from there it runs in a fairly straight line, crossing three large granite stiles before reaching Treen, where there are two smaller stiles. On the right are coastguard cottages, one bearing a George VI emblem.

Continue to the main road for the Hotel, which has on offer a surprising range of dishes. In deference to the setting we (that is, my late wife Viv and I, back in 1993) chose "Smoked Gurnard Crumble", and I followed that with "Thunder and Lightning", which included ice cream, black treacle, clotted cream and gin... Luckily our car was parked outside, and we decided against any further walking! If you have a walk back to Zennor to complete, however, **return to the coast path, either by the same route or by the shorter, unofficial route described next.**

For this, take the wide, partially concreted track which curves right as it leaves Treen: there is a metal gate at the start, with a rudimentary stile beside it. A waymark yellow arrow appears to confirm that this is a right of way, though not shown as such on the OS maps; it is certainly used by many walkers, and I think you are very unlikely to be challenged if you follow suit - but the decision is yours. (The maps indicate a field path, but this seems to have fallen out of use: in 2004 we failed to find any trace of it at the Treen end.) The wide track - actually a drive serving a few dwellings - winds its way down to the Gurnard's Head Mine engine house, then down a little further to where the coast path crosses. Turn right on that for Carnelloe and Zennor.

At Carnelloe follow the signs indicating the coast path and Zennor. On the east side of the headland you have quite a strenuous climb above Veor Cove. ("Veor" is derived from the Cornish word for "big", so "Veor Cove" means the same as "Porthmeor" nearby and also "Porthbeor" in the Roseland.) A mine called Wheal Veor (a very small mine, despite its name!) is mentioned by Alison Symons: she refers to the horse whim it employed, and says its "central stone, with a hole in the middle, is still visible, as is the small shelter hewn out of solid rock where the young lad, who kept the horse moving, could sit protected from the westerly gales." Nearby was the smelting works I mentioned earlier.

After Veor Cove the path runs fairly level above the gently sloping cliffs, out of which rise great rocky stacks, then makes a descent above Pendour ("head of the water") Cove, famous for its association with the legendary Zennor mermaid. A seat at the top of the slope gives a good opportunity to study the massive headland, cut into by a deep, narrow cleft known as Horseback Zawn from the shape of the ridge that divides it from the sea; and also the valley, where the ruins of an old watermill are overshadowed by the modern bungalow ("Carn Cobba") that looks so out of place in this setting. Eglosmeor (Great Church) Mill, referred to in *Tremedda Days* as Steven's Mill, was destroyed by the flood of 12th November 1894 which did so much damage in local mines such as Wheal Cock (Botallack). A battery of stamps was also sited close to the mill at one time.

Zennor Head

As you walk down towards the stream there is a glimpse of Zennor church. A footbridge provides a fine view of what in winter was a torrent roaring around and over massive granite boulders. **Then comes a long climb up a flight of steps, with a welcome seat part-way up, ending at a T-junction where you could turn right for Zennor or complete the recommended walk by turning left for Zennor Head.**

5 Fixed to the rocky outcrop above the tip of the headland is a plaque giving some information about the presentation of this place to the National Trust in 1953. A little further on there is a second such outcrop, and beside that what looks like evidence of an early mining venture, a long, shallow trench running inland from near the cliff edge. Much of the ground around this spot seems to have been disturbed in a way characteristic of many small-scale shallow workings. **The path now descends and climbs again on the eastern side of the headland,** and just before it reaches a level path at the top, where there is a coast-path signpost, any doubts that this area has been mined are dispelled by the water-filled portal of an adit beside the path. According to Des Hannigan, in fact, the lower cliffs here are "riddled with adits" of tin and copper mines.

6 Turn right at the coast path sign to return to Zennor by the high path. Keep to the main path as it wanders among bracken and low scrub, and at the T-junction turn left on the wider path. After crossing a stile above the big bungalow, Carn Cobba, you are on a narrow road into Zennor. Keep straight on after passing the church to return to the car park.

WALK 12
ST IVES (HALSETOWN CHURCH), TREVAIL, RIVER COVE & THE CLIFFS
About 6 miles

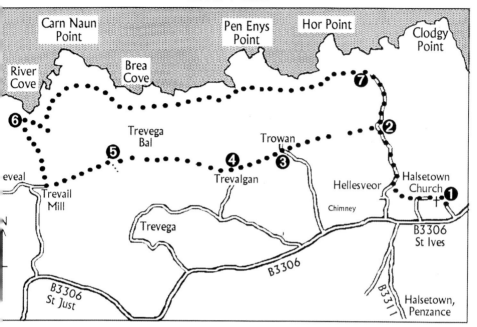

Reproduced by permission of Ordnance Survey on behalf of the Controller of Her Majesty's Stationery Office © Crown Copyright

This walk divides fairly equally into two very contrasting parts: field paths through quite flat farmland with fine inland views of the hills from Rosewall to Carn Galver; and a much more strenuous clifftop walk with equally fine coastal views, especially to the east. Between the two is a very attractive and unspoilt valley running down to the sea. The route passes through or close to the setts of at least five mines, one described by A.K.Hamilton Jenkin as "rich and important", two medium-sized enterprises and two that scarcely seem to have got properly under way.

In the winter this was definitely a walk to take your wellies on: cattle had churned up most gateways and many of the farm lanes into sticky mud at least ankle-deep; some of the farms seemed to he having a bumper slurry-making season, and even on the coast path there were some very boggy stretches. Things may be very different in July; but I wouldn't bank on it. Ideally take a good stout pair of walking boots too, because this is in general a pretty rough and rocky part of the coast. A stick

141

would also be useful to help with a few awkward, perhaps overgrown stiles. There is no pub or shop along the way.

Volume 5 of *Exploring Cornish Mines* includes a guided tour of the various sites occupied by the important group of mines, St Ives Consols. These include not only the part of St Ives where this walk starts and ends, but also Rosewall Hill and the Nancledra area. A less detailed account of a walk in part of the same territory is in *A View from Trencrom,* along with a walk in St Ives itself, exploring the fascinating history of the town.

There is a fairly large car park at Halsetown church - which, please note, is NOT in Halsetown! To drive to it, take the St Just / Land's End road out of St Ives (B3306). As you approach the edge of the town you will see the church, with its distinctive gabled spire, on your right, and the clearly signed side road leading to it comes about a quarter of a mile before the junction with the Penzance road (B3311). The car park is behind the church at the right-hand side as you drive up to it.

HALSETOWN CHURCH, ST. J0HN'S-IN-THE-FIELDS

An outline of the story of how Halsetown (say "Hallstown") came to be created at the time of the 1832 electoral reform act is given in "A View from Trencrom"; if you have not, as they say, "invested" in that, read the very detailed history of St John's on sale in the church, which not only tells the story but adds human flesh to the bare bones. Several of the mines nearby, such as St Ives Consols and Giew (near Nancledra), had a large and expanding work force during the second quarter of the 19th century, so the need for an Anglican church closer than St Ives came increasingly to be felt. Permission for Halsetown, with the addition of nearby hamlets such as Hellesvean and Hellesveor, to be constituted a separate parish was granted in 1846. The obvious choice of architect for the new church and vicarage was J.P. St Aubyn, who seems to have played a leading part in the "restoration" of almost every medieval church in Cornwall, much to the disgust of Sir John Betjeman and others. Even Betjeman, however, found St John's "impressive" - certainly it is distinctive, and manages to feel spacious yet friendly inside, though the friendliness is partly a result of decisions within the last thirty years to remove the pews and pulpit, carpet the entire floor and move the altar to a central position.

Why build the church so far from the village? The reason is said to be that all the landowners there were "chapel" and no-one would sell land to the Anglicans! And what about the fields? In fact the site chosen was indeed very rural at the time. St Ives has expanded to enclose it, and has shifted its centre of gravity in this direction to such an extent that Halsetown parish now has a larger population than St Ives.

1 The path runs behind the church car park: access to it is at the right-hand corner, up a few steps and under a low arch. Turn left on the path, which soon brings you to a pretty group of cottages. Continue almost straight ahead, following a footpath sign, beside one of the cottages. A few steps lead up into a field. A short distance to the left now is Consols Farm. The farmhouse was formerly the count house of St Ives Consols mine.

ST IVES CONSOLS

"Then we came to a mine called St Ives Consols, and the works, rattling, clanking, clumping, at 'stamping' and 'streaming' tin." So wrote Francis Kilvert in his diary on 29th July, 1870. Five years earlier, Thomas Spargo had noted, "The late Mr James Halse made a fortune out of this mine." It was easily the most productive one in the area explored on this walk: Collins estimates the value of the tin and copper raised between 1827 and 1892 as just over a million pounds, and states that for most of this period the mine employed between 300 and 500 people. An unusual feature of the mine was the so-called "carbonas", great irregular masses of tin ore. The largest, at a depth of 77 fathoms below adit, when extracted left caverns as much as 70 feet in height and width. These caverns had to be supported with, as Cyril Noall puts it, "absolute forests" of wooden beams and pillars, and the mine suffered a considerable blow in 1844 when the supports in the Great Carbona were accidentally set alight through the carelessness of a miner who left his candle stuck to one of the roof timbers. The fire burnt on for six weeks.

The mine, under various names, had a long life: Hamilton Jenkin writes of its being "re-started" in 1818 - and its final "re-start" was 90 years later, when a new company operated it in conjunction with three neighbouring mines: Rosewall Hill and Ransome United, Trenwith and Giew. This operation ceased in 1915 in the original St Ives Consols section, but continued till 1923 at Giew, whose big pumping-engine house at Frank's Shaft still dominates the countryside near the Engine Inn at Cripplesease. Walks visiting the Rosewall mines and Giew are included in "A View from Trencrom". A larger reproduction of the 1860s photograph is in Lena and Donald Bray's "St Ives Heritage", which also includes interesting personal reminiscences connected with mining in the St Ives area early this century.

A busy scene at the St Ives Consols dressing floors, about 1860

Here turn right, keep to the field-edge for a few yards, then follow the obvious path diagonally across the field. When you reach the hedge, don't cross the stile ahead (the path this leads to is in too poor a condition to be recommended). Instead, continue with the hedge on your left, past the remains of a kissing-gate, and then cross the large stile (if that's the word for it) on the left beside a metal farm gate. This brings you to a farm track; turn right on that and continue for nearly half a mile.

2 Cross the stile on the left, beside another metal farm gate. The path - which is, in fact, the "Church Road" mentioned on page 113 - runs in a fairly straight line to Trowan Farm. It keeps near the hedge on the

right at first, then passes through a series of gaps, some with gates, in field boundaries. At most of these there is a stile or the remains of one, and on the left side of each there used to be a wooden post painted black-and-white; many of these posts are still there, but the paint has faded. Look left to see Rosewall Hill, recognisable by the two mine stacks on its left-hand slope. The chimney closer, also on your left, is a relic of St Ives Wheal Allen. **After crossing the last stile, opposite Trowan farmhouse, turn left for a couple of yards, then right: there are two footpath signs on farm buildings.**

ST IVES WHEAL ALLEN

Dr Hamilton Jenkin quotes from a document dated 1786 which refers to the workings of Wheal Allen as already "old". During the following century the mine invested in steam engines for pumping and stamping, but it relied entirely on horses for winding, like so many smaller, shallow concerns. Dr Jenkin paints a vivid picture of the two horses at each of the three whims as they "plodded round and round the whim plats almost without attention, the boy drivers sitting half asleep on the capstan bars". St Ives Wheal Allen appears to have closed in 1868: its machinery was advertised for sale in the "West Briton" on 23rd April. Little if anything remains on the surface to tell of this mine's existence save the lonely stack, from a 30" pumping engine.

3 You have two stiles to cross within a few yards. From here to Trevalgan Farm the path again runs quite straight; there are four more stiles, the last of them just to the right of the farm buildings. The path doesn't pass through the farmyard, but keeps right of that, crossing a very boggy patch with the aid of a few stepping-stones.

4 Just beyond the farmhouse there are two stiles side-by-side; they are in the space between a garage on the left and a low building on the right, which was under construction early in 2004. (This looks like the latest addition to the holiday accommodation advertised by Trevalgan. Such "diversification" is increasingly necessary for Cornish farms.) **Cross the right-hand stile. Keep by the hedge on your left as it curves right, and go through the second gateway on your left. Now head slightly right of the stamps-engine house of Trevega Bal, cutting off the left-hand corner of the field, and cross the stile just beyond the point where the stone hedge juts out.**

WALK 12
TREVEGA BAL

The lonely ruins of the Trevega Bal stamps-engine house (on the skyline), as seen later in the walk

This mine appears in the records of Cornish mining under various names. Some if not all of the small enterprises which eventually combined as Trevega Bal were very old: the use of gunpowder for blasting in West Penwith is said to have been pioneered here as early as 1700. As the mine developed during the 19th century, the deepest workings were near the cliffs and under the sea at Brea Cove. It closed in 1871; according to Dr Jenkin it was "last investigated, in a half-hearted way, immediately prior to the 1914 war." Alison Symons (see Further Reading) states that early in the 20th century the "dirt" from the mine was drawn up by a "whipsaderry", that is a Whip-and-Derry (derrick), defined by W.G.Orchard as "A kibble drawn to the surface by a horse, the rope attaching one to the other, and simply passing over a pulley". It was then carted to the other side of the valley where there were water-powered stamps, but in the mine's last years the cart was replaced by an overhead cable system operated by a steam engine.

Now walk with the hedge on your left (the engine house should be straight ahead now), crossing two more stiles. The second, just left of a metal gate, is awkward to climb down on the far side. By now the view ahead is just beginning to reveal Carn Galver, emerging from behind Zennor Hill; and to your left between Rosewall and Trendrine Hills is the valley in which Towednack church is situated. Unsurprisingly, since it has a very low tower, we did not notice it from this distance. **The path**

146

goes on in the same line with the hedge now on your right, crossing six more stiles, the last of which brings you to a path between hedges. Here turn right and then almost immediately left. **The path to Trevail Mill, down in the valley, from here on is very clear.** At the point where you cross the stream there is a pond to the right - presumably the original mill pond. Des Hannigan's National Trust leaflet states that there were originally two mills at Trevail. The path runs right beside the mill house and then starts to climb towards Treveal - now basically a farm, but in the great days of mining it would, he says, have been a vigorous and well-populated hamlet.

5 **Having passed in front of the mill house - duckboards laid across the lawn - continue ahead for a few yards up the concreted drive, and immediately after the cattle grid take the path on the right, signed to River Cove.** The top part of the Treveal Valley is quite thickly wooded. Among the trees and down by the stream there are several small excavations, and one deeper hole with water flowing from it looks very much like an adit. Some of these features may have been created by Trevega Bal, but most are probably evidence of a much smaller concern called Wheal Cleveland, dating from the 1840s. Soon the trees come to an end - just beyond a rather magical spot where curvaceous, mossy branches of two trees overhang the stream and the path - and a beautiful view of the little valley opens up. It looks about as remote from industrial landscape as can be imagined, but the nearby mines made full use of the Treveal stream to drive stamps and supply buddles. **Continue ahead on the path down the western side of the valley till you reach the coast path near the cliff edge.**

6 **Turn right on that. It winds down to the valley bottom, where there is a stone footbridge.**

The side path to the rocks overlooking River Cove is worth a short diversion: this is often a good vantage point for watching seals. The long depression that starts as the Trevail Valley and the gap between Rosewall and Trendrine Hills continues as the Red River Valley via Towednack, Nancledra and Crowlas almost as far as Marazion, so that from a few miles out to sea it appears that all the land to the west is an island: C. Lewis Hind in *Days in Cornwall* (1907) writes that seamen call River Cove "the Open Gate". I presume the whole valley would have been navigable four million years ago, when the sea level was about 130m higher than now, if there had been anyone around then to sail it.

The coast path itself now takes you on a long climb up to the top of
Treveal Cliff, above Carn Naun Point - an exceptionally bare, bleak
spot, but what a view it commands! Pendeen Watch (about 7 miles) cuts
off the view south-west, but once you reach the trig. point column you
can look east to Godrevy lighthouse (about 6 m.), St Agnes Beacon (just
over 13 m.), Kelsey Head near Newquay (c. 22 m.) and in clear conditions
Trevose Head near Padstow (c. 32 m.). Quite close at hand is the Trevega
stamps-engine house, and when you reach the rocky outcrop above Brea
Cove you will be able to see another ruined mine building part-way down
the sloping cliff. This was a pumping-engine house, and the mouth of
the shaft from which it pumped is probably on the flat area just below it.
At the bottom of the cliff, just above high-water mark, are the portals of
several adits; the same mine also had a much longer adit - nearly half a
mile - which drained into the sea at River Cove.

**The next big headland is Pen Enys ("Island Head") Point; before
reaching that the path runs close to the head of the impressive zawn
called Polgassick Cove, where wooden duckboarding and concrete
paving slabs have been laid down to help you across one of the many
boggy patches on this stretch of cliff.** "Polgassick" means "mare's pool";
certainly there's plenty of water to take the horse to up here! **Beyond a**

Some of the spectacular coastal scenery on this walk

kissing gate the path crosses two streams as it cuts across the neck of the headland. Ahead now is Hor ("Ram") Point - which may take you longer to reach than you expect, since this part of the cliff path is particularly rough underfoot. The coast path again runs well inland of the point itself, but there is a clear path out to it on the far (eastern) side, and this is well worth the diversion if old mines interest you.

Hor copper mine occupies only the tiniest of niches in mining history, but it has left a massive shaft (blocked a few feet down) in a very spectacular situation. The base of a masonry wall rests precariously on the edge of the shaft, with fallen blocks scattered among the mine waste nearby. A note in Dr Jenkin's *The Cornish Miner* (1927) mentions "Captain Martin Dunn's engine-house at Hor Bal". Old people could remember that 16 horses had to be used to manoeuvre the bob along the twisting, narrow lane. "It took several days to get it down, and all the neighbourhood turned out to see it." Just above the shaft is a circular "plat" about 35 feet in diameter, possibly the site of a horse whim. Des Hannigan tells the story of how in 1957 the National Trust and the owner of Hor Point combined to foil a plan by St Ives Town Council to purchase the headland compulsorily and turn it into a garbage tip.

Ruins of the engine house perched on the edge of its shaft on Hor Point

Continue on the coast path till you reach a sign indicating St Ives to the left; close by is the National Trust Hellesveor Cliff sign.

7 Here leave the coast path, continuing ahead along a farm lane or track between hedges. After about a quarter of a mile there is a wooden gate, and soon after that the main inland path between Zennor and St Ives crosses. The rest of the walk retraces your steps at the start, but just in case you've forgotten: not far beyond a house (Pedn-an-Vounder, "end of the lane"), the track turns quite sharply to the right. At that point, go through the gap or over the "stile" on the left. Walk beside the hedge on your right, past the remains of a kissing-gate, a few more yards beside the hedge and then diagonally left across the field. The path on your left beside a house soon returns you to St John's-in-the-Fields.

SOME MINING TERMS

This book is written with the interested general reader in mind, rather than those who have made a special study of mining in Cornwall. Although some explanations of technical terms are included in the main text, I think a brief glossary may prove helpful. Please bear in mind, however, that these are very simplified explanations: several of these words have formed the basis of lengthy articles and even whole books. The illustrations in this section, apart from those of the buddle and horse whims, are taken from the Perran Foundry catalogue dating from the early 1870s, by courtesy of the Trevithick Society.

ADIT A drainage channel with its mouth or **PORTAL** in a valley or on a hillside or cliff face. In deep mines the water had to be raised by pumping to the level of the adit; this is why statistics often state the depth of a mine "below adit". Adits also often doubled as shafts by following the metal **LODE** (vein), and in some cases provided access for the miners.

BAL An area of tin-working. Mines named Bal tend to be older than those called **WHEAL** or **HUEL**, though this is certainly not a hard-and-fast rule. Oliver Padel suggests that a Bal was generally a group of workings, especially on the surface, whereas a Wheal was a specific tin-work.

BEAM ENGINE Thomas Newcomen of Dartmouth (1663-1729) was the first to develop a steam engine which could be used for pumping water up from the mines. The cylinder was placed vertically, and the piston was chained to one end of a massive wooden or cast iron beam or **BOB**, pivoted on a strong wall, known as the **BOB WALL**. The other end overhung the

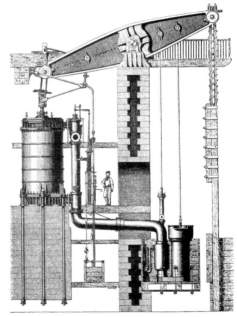

A typical large steam pumping engine. This one was made for Poldice Mine, near St Day.

151

mine shaft and was attached by long rods to the pump at the bottom. In deep shafts the pitwork, as it was called, would have been too heavy for the beam to lift without the aid of at least one **BALANCE BOB.** Balance bobs were small beams with one end attached to the pump rod and the other heavily weighted: when the rod descended the balance bob's weight prevented it from falling too quickly, and when it rose the weight helped it up. In the 1770s James Watt and Matthew Boulton began manufacturing an improved engine, and James Pickard modified beam engines to produce rotative motion, used mainly for driving the whim and stamps. (See the entries on those.) Early in the 19th century, great improvements were brought by the use of high-pressure steam; the research and inventions of Richard Trevithick (1771-1833) made an important contribution here, but many other engineers also played a significant part. The size of each engine was expressed in terms of the diameter of its cylinder: 45", 90", etc.

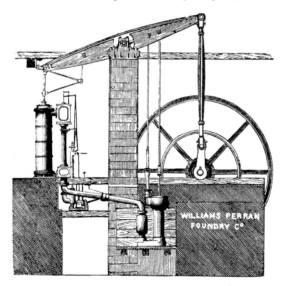

A rotative beam engine, normally used for winding or for driving stamps; also sometimes for pumping, but a small engine of this type would not be adequate for pumping large quantities of water from great depths.

BUDDLE A device for concentrating ore by means of gravity. Early buddles were rectangular, but in the 19th century most were circular; water containing the ore which had been reduced to a fine powder in the stamps was fed to the centre of a **CONVEX BUDDLE** or the sides of a **CONCAVE** one, and rotating brushes were used to ensure that the heaviest, metal-bearing particles settled closest to the inlet point. A more

A restored convex buddle at Blue Hills Tin Streams, near St Agnes

sophisticated form of buddle called a **ROUND FRAME** came into use in Cornwall in the 1870s. In this the bowl rather than the brushes rotated.

BURROW or **DUMP** A heap of mine waste (**DEADS** or **ATTLE**) - often very useful now as evidence of the mine's production. The burrows of many old mines have been "worked over" for valuable minerals which can be recovered by improved techniques.

CALCINER (pronounced "cal-sign-er") A furnace in which ore was roasted in order to drive off impurities such as arsenic and sulphur. If the arsenic was wanted, the fumes were passed though a long, zigzag flue known as a **LAMBRETH** (labyrinth), from which the deposits were collected.

COFFIN, COFFEN or **GOFFEN** One of many terms used for mining on the surface. A coffin or **GUNNIS** is a narrow, slot-like excavation; where a broader, quarry-like pit was dug the term used was **OPENWORK** or **BEAM**. The word **STOPE** normally means an excavated area underground, but is also sometimes used of surface workings.

COUNT HOUSE The mine's office.

DRESSING FLOOR The area where the ore was prepared for smelting.

DRY A building where mine workers changed their clothes; some dries also had washing and/or bathing facilities. Photos exist of the big pipes connected to engine boilers which heated the dry at Levant.

FATHOM Six feet.

FLAT-RODS Wooden or (usually) iron rods which were used to transfer power from a steam engine or waterwheel to a remote location.

LEAT An artificial watercourse. Where a leat was carried in a raised trough it was known as a **LAUNDER**.

MAN ENGINE An apparatus for raising and lowering men in a shaft, first used in Cornwall during the 1840s. Steps and hand-holds were fixed to a rod, or in some cases two rods, connected to an engine at surface. At Levant, which used the single-rod type, there were fixed platforms, about 18" square, at corresponding intervals in the shaft so that by stepping from rod to fixed platform or vice-versa at the instant they became level with one another, a miner could go up or down.

REVETMENT A wall built to support an earth bank.

SETT "The ground granted to a company of adventurers" (C. C. James) (**ADVENTURERS** were shareholders in a mining enterprise, but with unlimited liability.) The word "sett" was also used for the granite blocks used to carry rails.

STAMPS Cornish Stamps machines were used to crush the small lumps of ore into material like sand in texture. Heavy timber or iron lifters with iron "heads" at the bottom were raised by cams on a rotating axle,

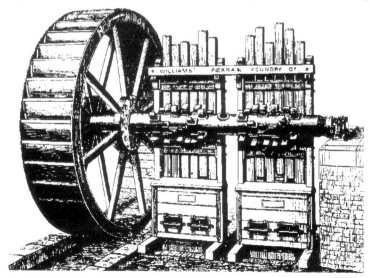

and fell on the ore, fed into a box beneath. Small stamps were usually powered by water-wheels, as in the picture, and larger ones by steam engines. **CALIFORNIAN STAMPS** began to supersede the Cornish variety late in the 19th century. Developed in the Californian goldfields, they employed heavier heads, which rotated, thus reducing wear and enabling a much greater output of crushed ore.

STREAMING The normal method of winning tin before deep mining became possible. **ALLUVIAL TIN** washed down into valleys and buried under silt was exposed, originally by shovel and barrow; the tin-bearing gravel was then sorted and washed, and the waste material used to back-fill the excavated area. Nowadays, earth-movers and lorries do the work.

WHIM A machine for raising or lowering ore or other heavy materials - and sometimes men. The earliest whims were operated by human beings or horses, walking round and round a flat circular area called a **WHIM PLAT** turning a wooden drum or capstan, around which was wound the cable attached to the **KIBBLE** or bucket. Some **HORSE WHIMS** continued in use till the 20th century, but the whims in deep mines were driven by steam engines. An improvement on kibbles were the steel containers called **SKIPS**; these were sometimes equipped with wheels and drawn up and down the rails of a **SKIP ROAD**.

Horse whims, from Agricola's "De Re Metallica" (1556). Those in Cornwall were either in the open air or protected from the elements in a round building, often with a thatched roof, as shown (right) in Pryce's "Mineralogia Cornubiensis" (1778).

FURTHER READING

Here are some of the books I have found most interesting and useful; details of a few others are given in the walk descriptions. The standard works on Cornish mining (Pryce, Collins, Dines, Hamilton Jenkin, Ordish, Barton, Trounson) are omitted here, but were of course consulted. Many of the books listed are out of print, but may be found in local libraries and secondhand-book shops.

Beaufort-Murphy, Mary (ed.), *West Penwith at the Time of Charles II* (Penwith Local History Group, 1998)

Bere, Rennie, *The Nature of Cornwall* (Barracuda, 1982)

Blight, J.T., *A Week at the Land's End* (1873, reprinted 1973)

"Bosanketh, Edward" (R.E.Boyns), *Tin, A Novel* (1888; new edition published by Justin Brooke, 1998)

Bray, Lena & Donald, *St Ives Heritage* (Truran,1981; revised edition, Landfall Publications, 1992)

Brown, Kenneth & Acton, Bob, *Exploring Cornish Mines*, Volumes 1,2,3 & 5 (Landfall Publications, 1994-2001)

Brunton, Alan, *Will I Fly Again?* (Orchard Publications, 1993)

Buck, Colin & Berry, Eric, *St Just Town Survey* (Cornwall Archaeological Unit, 1996)

Buller, John, *A Statistical Account of the Parish of Saint Just ...* (1840; facsimile edition 1983, Dyllansow Truran)

Chesher, Veronica & Palmer, June (eds), *Three Hundred Years on Penwith Farms* (Penwith Local History Group, 1994)

Cook, Judith, *When I set out for Lyonesse ... Cornish Walks and Legends* (Alison Hodge, 1984)

Cooke, Ian McNeil, *Journey to the Stones* (Men-an-Tol Studio, 2nd edition 1996)

Cooke, Ian McNeil, *Mother and Sun: The Cornish Fogou* (Men-an-Tol Studio, 1993)

Cooke, Ian McNeil, *Antiquities of West Cornwall* (four pocket guides) (Men-an-Tol Studio, 1989-91)

Corin, John, *Levant - A Champion Cornish Mine* (Trevithick Society, 1992)

Corin, John, *Sennen Cove and its Lifeboat* (RNLI Sennen Cove, 1985)

Deane, Tony & Shaw, Tony, *The Folklore of Cornwall* (Batsford, 1975)

Demuth, Averil (ed.), *The Minack Open-Air Theatre* (David & Charles, 1968)

Dundrow, Michael et al, *Madron's Story* (Bossiney, 2001)

Edmonds, Richard, *The Land's End District* (J.R.Smith, 1862)

Goode, Tony, *Land's End* and *St Ives to Cape Cornwall* (two "Holiday Geology Guide" laminated leaflets) (British Geological Survey, 1995)

FURTHER READING

Goode,Tony, Holder,Martin & Leveridge,Brian, *West Cornwall, A Landscape for Leisure* (British Geological Survey, 1996)

Hannigan, Des, National Trust *Coast of Cornwall* leaflets Nos 10 &11

Hannigan, Des, *Wildlife Walkabouts: Land's End Peninsula, Cornwall* (Wayside Books, 1986)

Hawker, Oliver, *Land's End* (Halsgrove, 2003)

Hockin, J.R.A., *Walking in Cornwall* (Methuen, 1936)

Hocking, Mary, *Safari West* (Churchtown Technology, 1996)

Hosking, Jim, *People, Places & Past Events in St Buryan* (Author, 2002)

Hudson, W.H., *The Land's End, A Naturalist's Impressions in West Cornwall* (Dent, 1908)

Hunt, Robert, *Popular Romances of the West of England* (Chatto & Windus, 1881)

Jennings, H.R. *Notes on the History of Madron, Morvah and Penzance* (1936)

Johnson, Nicholas & Rose, Peter, *Cornwall's Archaeological Heritage* (Twelveheads, 1990)

Joseph, Peter, *Mining Accidents in the St Just District 1831-1914* (Trevithick Society, 1999)

Lane-Davies, A., *Holy Wells of Cornwall* (Federation of Old Cornwall Societies, 1970)

Langdon, Andrew, *Stone Crosses in West Penwith* (The Federation of Old Cornwall Societies, 1997)

Larn, Richard & Carter, Clive, *Cornish Shipwrecks - The South Coast* (David & Charles, 1969)

Leggatt, P.O. & D.V., *The Healing Wells* (Truran, 1987)

Leifchild, J.R., *Cornwall, Its Mines & Miners* (1855; reprinted 1968)

Luck, Liz, *South Cornish Harbours* (A & C Black, 1988)

Meyrick, J., *A Pilgrim's Guide to the Holy Wells of Cornwall* (Author, 1982)

Mitchell, Susie, *Recollections of Lamorna* (Author, 1977)

Nankervis, Jean, *Wicca, A Farm in West Cornwall* (author, revised edition 1991)

Nicholas, Edith M., *St Just & Pendeen* (Old Cornwall Society, 1968)

Noall, Cyril, *Botallack* (D.B.Barton, 1972)

Noall, Cyril, *Cornish Mine Disasters* (Truran, 1989)

Noall, Cyril, *The Illustrated Past: Penwith* (Barracuda, 1978)

Noall, Cyril, *Levant - The Mine beneath the Sea* (D.B.Barton, 1970)

Noall, Cyril, *The St Ives Mining District* (Truran, 1982)

Noall, Cyril, *The St Just Mining District* (D.B.Barton, 1973)

Orchard, W.G., *A Glossary of Mining Terms* (Truran, 1991)

Packer, J.E., *Messages under the Sea* (Author, 1981)

FURTHER READING

Packer, J.E., *The Porthcurno Handbook* (Author, undated)

Packer, J.E., *The Spies at Wireless Point* (Author, 1991)

Padel, O.J., *Cornish Place-Name Elements* (English Place-Name Society, 1985)

Padel, O.J., *A Popular Dictionary of Cornish Place-Names* (Alison Hodge, 1988)

Paris, Dr.J.A., *A Guide to the Mount's Bay and the Land's End* (Phillips, 1824)

Pendeen Art Group, *Pendeen Past & Present* (1995)

Pender, Nettie M., *Mousehole, History and Recollections* (S. Johns, 1985)

"Penhale, Jack" (Raymond Harry), *The Mine under the Sea* (Lake, 1962)

"Penwith, John" (Joe Martin), *Leaves from a Cornish Notebook* (The Cornish Library, Penzance, undated)

Perry, Margaret E., *Mousehole, A Brief History* (Author, 1998)

Priestland, Gerald & Sylvia, *West of Hayle River* (Wildwood House, 1980, reprinted as *Priestlands' Cornwall*, Grafton, 1992)

Quiller-Couch, M. & L., *Ancient and Holy Wells of Cornwall* (Clark, 1894)

Sagar-Fenton, Michael, *About Penzance, Newlyn & Mousehole* (Bossiney, 2000)

Sagar-Fenton, Michael, *Penlee, The Loss of a Lifeboat* (Bossiney, 1991)

Sharpe, Adam, *St Just - An Archaeological Survey of the Mining District* (Cornwall Archaeological Unit, 1992)

Sinclair, David J., *St Just Mining Area* (Phoenix Project, 1992)

Stanier, Peter, *Cornwall's Geological Heritage* (Twelveheads, 1990)

Stanier, Peter, *The Work of Giants, Great Granite Rocks of Cornwall and Scilly (*St Ives Printing & Publishing Company, 1988)

Symons, Alison, *Tremedda Days, A View of Zennor 1900-1944* (Tabb House 1992)

Tarrant, Michael, *Cornwall's Lighthouse Heritage* (Twelveheads, 1990)

Tregenza, Douglas, *Departed Days: Mousehole Remembered* (Truran, 1984)

Tregenza, Leo, *Harbour Village* (Mousehole) (William Kimber, 1977)

Weatherhill, Craig, *Belerion, Ancient Sites of Land's End* (Alison Hodge, 1981)

Weatherhill, Craig, *Cornish Place Names & Language* (Sigma, 1995)

Weatherhill, Craig & Devereux, Paul, *Myths and Legends of Cornwall* (Sigma, 1994)

Williams, Douglas, *Mount's Bay* (Bossiney, 1984)

Williams, Michael, *Around & About Land's End* (Bossiney, 1997)

Williams, Michael, *Around Land's End* (Bossiney, 1983)

Yglesias, Dorothy, *The Cry of a Bird* and *In Answer to the Cry* (William Kimber, 1962 & 1975)

OTHER LANDFALL BOOKS

  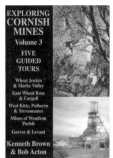 

The *Exploring Cornish Mines* series provides guided tours of the surface remains of the most interesting and important mines in the county. All except Volume 4 include at least one walk in West Penwith: Vol. 1, Botallack and neighbouring mines; Vol. 2, Ding Dong; Vol. 3, Geevor & Levant; Vol. 5, St Ives Consols, St Just United & Cape Cornwall. Each volume is priced £8.25.

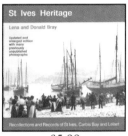

 £5.99

Cornwall during and after World War 2 - two of Landfall's best-sellers, price £6.99 each.

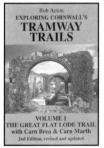 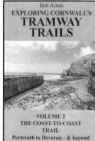

Guides to the Mineral Tramways Project routes (long-distance trails open to cyclists and horse-riders, plus many walks) and the places of interest along the way. Fully illustrated with maps and photographs, old and new. Both books have sections of full-colour photos.
Price £7.50 each.

Also available:

A History of Truro (3 volumes), by Viv and Bob Acton
The Bells of Truro (autobiography), by Phyllis Jones
Launceston, Some Pages in History, by Joan Rendell
Enjoy Falmouth, by Bob Acton & Peter Gilson
Newquay's Pictorial Past (old photographs)
Write or ring for Landfall's current list.

OTHER LANDFALL WALKS BOOKS

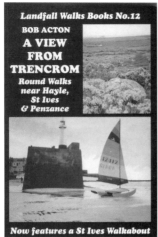

This book details most of the other interesting and attractive walks West Penwith offers. "Historical Walkabouts" in St Ives and Hayle are included, along with country walks taking in Gulval, Castle-an-Dinas, Chysauster ancient village, Ludgvan, Cripplesease, Nancledra, Prussia Cove, Perranuthnoe, St Hilary, Goldsithney, St Erth, Gwinear, Phillack, Lelant, Carbis Bay, Halsetown, Towednack, Rosewall Hill and the fine viewpoint which overlooks all this landscape, Trencrom. Like *Around Land's End*, it is illustrated and gives plenty of detail on points of interest.

110 pages, price £3.99

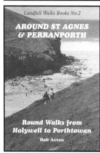

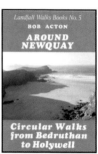

Shown here are the rest of the currently available books in the series. All are priced £3.99 except *Around the Fal* (£4.50), *Around the River Fowey* (£4.50) and *From the Roseland to St Austell Bay* (£4.95).

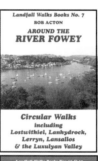

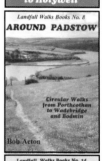

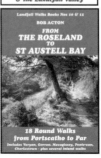